GW00733754

More Water With It

Cliff Parker

SPHERE BOOKS LIMITED

SPHERE BOOKS LTD

Penguin Books Ltd, 27 Wrights Lane, London W8 5TZ (Publishing and Editorial)
and Harmondsworth, Middlesex, England (Distribution and Warehousing)
Viking Penguin Inc., 40 West 23rd Street, New York, New York 10010, USA
Penguin Books Australia Ltd, Ringwood, Victoria, Australia
Penguin Books Canada Ltd, 2801 John Street, Markham, Ontario, Canada L3R 1B
Penguin Books (NZ) Ltd, 182–190 Wairau Road, Auckland 10, New Zealand

First published in Great Britain by Sphere Books Ltd 1987

Printed and bound in Great Britain by
Richard Clay Ltd, Bungay, Suffolk
Filmset in 11/12½ pt Baskerville

Contents

About this book

More Water With It is another collection of Cliff Parker's stirring sagas of angling folk, based on pieces originally published in angling journals who are happy to disclaim all responsibility.

Plus, unabridged and unexpurgated, *Uncle Clifford's Worry Corner* – twelve months of Uncle Clifford's sage advice to Worried Blue Eyes, a distraught young lady unwise enough (some say daft enough) to become romantically involved with a dedicated angler.

Are anglers as bad as they are painted? Are they as anti-social, sexist, chauvinistic, misanthropic, boozy, scruffy and untruthful as their popular image? Read this book and find out.

Gad, if that's *all* they were . . .

Assegai that did it

A dreadful cold spell set in, courtesy of winds from Siberia, which meant that I didn't get much fishing done for a couple of weeks in January – partly because it was difficult to get the bait through three inches of ice on the Grand Union, but mainly because I'm a coward. No way was I going to risk life, limb, nose and naughty bits by sitting around for eight hours in that lot.

I did, however, inspect the water – or attempt to inspect it, because it was under all that ice and a further layer of snow. But even the attempt was a mistake.

I was encouraged to venture out by Tactful Tetters, who rang up to say he'd meet me in the *Three Horseshoes*, an Old English hostelry near the lock, where I might discover something to my advantage.

Off I set, and was doing all right, waddling along the towpath in my olive-green Superman wellies, when my feet shot from under me on the ice and I went straight down on my bum. Didn't half hurt.

Nothing to worry about. Just the annual event of slipping on the ice and doing damage to my coccyx. 'Wash your mouth out with soap,' says Dearly Beloved. 'I'm not having language like that in front of the children.'

What happens when I bruise my coccyx, apart from its bringing the tears to my eyes, is that I get an instant funny walk. Stiff-legged and slow, just like the Frankenstein monster. It looked like being one of those days.

(A tip from Scandinavia is that if you wish to avoid falling flat on your back when walking on ice, you just turn your toes inwards. Then you fall flat on your face.)

. . . At the *Three Horseshoes* I was greeted by Tetters. He's not known as Tactful for nothing.

'You've got a funny walk, our Clifford,' he said. 'Couldn't you wait?'

'*Very* droll,' I said, through both my gritted teeth. 'I slipped on the towpath and I think I've done my coccyx in. Again.'

'Funny things, coccyxes,' said Tetters. 'Once you damage them, you never get right. I knew a chap who was in agony for years.'

'Thanks a bunch,' I said. 'And then what happened? A miracle cure?'

'No,' said Tetters. 'He died. Anyway, I've got a prezzie for you. The Assegai.'

Scuffling under the bench, he produced a fearsome looking spear, seven feet long and with a wicked, razor-sharp point.

I should explain that the title of my great novel, when I get round to writing it, will be *Kindly Remove That Assegai from the Head of My Friend*. It was inspired by something which happened at a party to Mad Mac (ol' buddy and dead liability), but it's too complicated to go into here.

Anyway, I'd mentioned it to Tetters who just happened to have an assegai he'd picked up some years back.

'You can have it,' he said.

'Are you sure?'

'Positive. I don't use it much at all these days.'

So I left the pub, the Frankenstein walk accentuated by a few pints and a large Scotch, clutching the assegai and hoping that the local constabulary would be relaxing their usual vigilance. They are possibly not too keen on blokes with funny walks lurching about clutching seven-foot assegais.

(Now is the time, if ever, to get rid of the Zulu identity parade joke: '*Assegai that did it*'.)

I had this feeling of impending doom. That something dreadful was going to happen before I got home. Almost immediately there was an omen.

In a field by the towpath was a bloke lying down in the snow. An angler, to judge by the basket, nets and rod cases that were strewn about him. (I should have been a detective. Not a lot escapes me.)

'Gad,' I thought, 'a fellow piscator in distress. Lucky I happened along.'

So I climbed very painfully over a stile and approached him.

'Are you all right?' I asked. 'Anything I can do?'

2

He sat bolt upright, gathered a double handful of snow, and tipped it all over his head.

'Tee-hee,' he went. 'Tee-hee. Ho-ho. Har-har-har . . .'

Then he rolled over onto his stomach and ploughed through the drifts with a very impressive crawl stroke.

From this I deduced that I had run into (a) the local loony; (b) an angler whose brain had been turned by the conditions on the canal, or (c) a drunk. Possibly all three: the local loony angler who had just got smashed out of his tinies on account of the inclement weather.

Whatever he was, there wasn't a lot I could do. He was swimming through the snow faster than I could peg-leg through it. In any case it wouldn't do to pursue him wielding a seven-foot assegai. So I returned to the towpath and staggered painfully on.

By this time a freezing fog had come down. It really was an eerie scene, with the odd ghostlike figure appearing suddenly from nowhere.

I was walking by the edge of a wood when I espied a motor-car in difficulties. It had been parked under the trees and now couldn't get out: wheels spinning like crazy in the drifted snow.

Good Deed Number Two coming up. I lumbered slowly and stiff-legged towards the car, just as the driver was getting out.

'Want a push?' I said.

'Aaargh!' screamed this woman. 'Aaaaaarrrrggghhh!'

'Please yourself,' I said, a bit abruptly, which is not like me at all. And, not wishing to be discovered by the vigilant constabulary with a seven-foot assegai in a wood with a screaming woman, lurched back into the fog.

* * *

'There are some people,' said Dearly Beloved as she massaged my head, to which the bobbly hat had frozen, 'who would say you are not all there. Staggering about like Frankenstein in the fog, accosting drunken anglers in snowdrifts, waving a damn great spear and putting the fear of God into lady motorists.

'And I'd be the first to agree with them,' she went on, as is

3

her wont. 'Even though I did promise to love, honour and obey. Now lift your chin up.'

'What for?'

'So I can oil the bolts in your neck . . .'

This sporting death

There are constant complaints from clubs and individual fisher-men about the poor TV coverage of angling.

I couldn't agree more. The TV companies must be barmy not to tap angling's potential – it's the biggest participant sport in the country, taking place often in the most photogenic surroundings, and packed with colourful personalities. (*Colourful personalities:* tellyspeak for raving loonies.)

There's certainly enough action to satisfy any television director. Even leaving out the match, the fracas at the average weigh-in makes wrestling on TV look like a prance around the maypole.

Certainly there is enough in angling for the commentators to keep up the interest from first thing in the morning to last thing at night. They do it in other sports by inspecting the pitch, showing fascinating shots of the rain that's stopped play for the past four hours, and interviewing players, managers and passing drunks.

So surely angling could top any sport for action and spec-tacle. Let's look ahead to the kind of enthralling TV coverage we could expect from an outside broadcast:

Commentator: And here we are at six o'clock on a cold and misty morning outside Parker Manor, home of Sludgethorpe's ace matchman, Cliff 'Dynamite Kid' Parker. Today is the needle match against Slagville Piscatorials, and Sludgethorpe are pinning their hopes on this shy, handsome, intelligent boy with magic in his match rod.

It's still very dark out here, but there have been signs of activity inside. The front door was opened about half an hour ago and a cat thrown out. So it shouldn't be long before the emergence of the Master himself.

Ah, the door has opened again. There's a crash of milk bottles ... And here comes Parker with that graceful and characteristic lurching gait.

What's this? The door has opened yet again and a tiny

female form runs after Parker. It's his Darling Daughter! Is she going to give him a big kiss for luck? No . . . she's handing him his butties which he doubtless forgot in the excitement of the moment.

Parker starts off again down the path. The front door has opened once more! This is certainly an exciting start to the day. A tall, youthful, hairy figure is calling to Parker. I can't quite catch it but it sounds like, 'Come back, you dozy old twit . . .' Ah yes, it's Parker's Number One Son, and he's handing his father his rods which he doubtless forgot in the excitement of the moment.

Now the Maestro has resumed his progress. What's this? My, my . . . the front door has opened one more time, and emerging is a distinguished looking lady with her hair in curlers . . . It's Parker's dearly beloved wife! What's she got for him, I wonder?

Ah, yes. His trousers, which he doubtless forgot in the excitement of the moment. I did think he was looking a bit goose-pimply between his anorak and welly tops. They've got the screens round him now. You can hear him grunting a little as he squeezes his muscular frame into the trousers – his lucky match trousers which after all these years are bound to be a little snug – and I think he's now ready. Yes, here he comes. We'll have a word.

Good morning, Cliff. May I be the first to wish you luck on this very important –

Parker (blearily): Eh? Yer wha'?

Commentator: Is there anything you'd like to say at the start of this very auspicious day?

Parker: Yes. Bugger off.

Commentator: What a wag he is, folks. A merry quip for every occasion. There he goes now, across the road to the bus stop. And here comes the bus. Parker steps aboard – what's this?

There seems to be some sort of altercation going on between him and the bus conductor. Now Parker's off the bus, seemingly without his gear. Ah, here it comes . . . Oh, dear – the basket's struck Parker on his bobbly hat and he's *down!* The bus is away, with the conductor throwing the last tin of maggots as it gathers speed.

What a dramatic start to the day. I hope it doesn't affect

6

Parker's performance. No – he's up . . . and there's another bus coming. This time he's aboard and safely away to the venue at Foundry Road Lock. We'll resume our transmission from there, folks, and meanwhile . . . back to the studio.

TIME PASSES

(AS WE SAY IN THE TRADE.)

Commentator: And here we are at Foundry Road Lock. Sorry about the delay, but the bus which Parker caught wasn't going to Foundry Road. However, he's walked back down the motorway and is here in time for the peg draw.

A few minutes to spare before the draw and Parker has been taken on one side by his trainer, Mad Mac, and his manager, Big McGinty. All three are in earnest and secret conference behind the lock keeper's shed, and something is passing between them. A plan of action, no doubt: a top security scenario for sweeping the board in today's Battle of the Giants.

No . . . It's a bottle of Scotch. What a confirmation of total confidence, if any were needed, in the Master's ability to make mincemeat of the opposition.

Here they go now . . . The Mighty Microbe, as he is fondly called – just look at those rounded shoulders glinting in the sun – and his stalwart seconds, known to matchmen the world over as the Titanic Two. Between then, Mad Mac and Big McGinty are unsinkable. What? Sorry, folks . . . a small correction from our director. Between them they'll sink anything. They'd sup the Grand Union dry if it was whisky.

[*Whispering:* Are you sure about that? There *is* such a thing as slander, you know. And McGinty *is* big. It's all right for you sitting back there in your little glass box. You don't have to

7

meet these – what? We're still on sound? Well, *you're* pulling the switches, ducky . . .]

Still there, folks? Ha, ha. A spot of crossed wires, it seems. These things happen in the best of . . . Ah, yes, the peg draw has taken place. Now what's Parker got? The favoured peg by the tripeworks outfall, as he had hoped? That, as McGinty was telling me only yesterday, they'd put all their money on?

No! Ohmygawd! Parker's got the bleachworks peg! This could upset the form no end! There are objections from Mad Mac and Big McGinty. Parker is forsaking his usual calm and aloof attitude and is making gestures with his rod rest towards the neutral chief steward. Mac and McGinty are already in what seem to be close encounters of the third kind with the Slagville First Reserves . . . all very large gentlemen from what I can make out.

There they go, all three of them – up in the air on the shoulders of the Slagvillians. Could this be an accolade from the Slagville team? An acknowledgement of the Sludgethorpe prowess? A lap of honour for our three, borne on high like conquering heroes as a tribute to their superior skill?

No. The three heroes have disappeared. And that splash seems to indicate the location. Just below the lock gates, I'd say. What a start to the match, folks! We're going to see some real action now! Yes, here they come . . . the Gruesome Threesome . . . soaking wet and crawling back onto the towpath with murder in their eyes. And all hell is breaking –

WE REGRET THAT
OWING TO A
TECHNICAL FAULT
WE ARE UNABLE TO
BRING YOU THE
REST OF OUR
PROGRAMME

Dear Worried Blue Eyes . . .

No newspaper or magazine is complete without its agony aunt, fount of all wisdom, soother of the fevered brow, comforter of the troubled in heart.

Most of the people who write to the agony aunts are women, generally younger women, who are possibly most vulnerable to the slings and arrows of outrageous fortune, more likely to be misused by the world in general.

Angling's agony column is no exception. Like all rugged outdoor activities, the sport makes heavy demands upon its practitioners, who in turn make heavy demands upon their nearest and dearest. Those who suffer most are the wives and girlfriends; the young, innocent, loving and trusting young ladies who give their all, or most of it, to an angler and then discover the stern tribute exacted by the noble art, the high price they have to pay for the privilege of sharing an angler's love with his longer-standing passion.

For centuries these long-suffering young ladies had no one to turn to; no caring, worldly-wise soul to advise them. Until the emergence of Uncle Clifford's Worry Corner.

Those who write to Uncle Clifford have heart-rending tales to tell. Of romantic and domestic misunderstandings brought about by the devotion to angling of the men in their lives; misunderstandings which threaten the very warp and weft, not to mention the woof, of their relationships. But, thanks to Uncle Clifford, they realise they are not alone; that there are three million or so women in the British Isles, and many more all over the world, suffering exactly as they are. Thanks to his comforting words, unparalleled sagacity and timely advice, their lot is made much easier.

Starting in the next chapter, and continuing at intervals throughout the book, we trace the month-by-month problems over a year in the life of Worried Blue Eyes (name and address supplied). Her story is typical of the many young girls today who have come across the harsh realities of life with an angler, and we see how Uncle Clifford's words of wisdom help her in relationships with both her angler boyfriend and her family.

'Why *Uncle* Clifford?' you may ask. 'Why not *Auntie* Clifford?'

Firstly, because Auntie Clifford would sound bloody silly. And get him talked about in the pub. Secondly because the special nature of the problems, calling as they do for a broad and deep knowledge of angling, needs a man to provide the answers.

The idea came to Uncle Clifford in a blinding flash of inspiration. He would place his million-dollar brain, and wisdom beyond his years, at the disposal of his fellow man – or woman, as the case may be. He was inspired by a deep-rooted need to be of service to humanity. To place whatever humble talents he had at the disposal of the troubled and oppressed. And because he was skint at the time.

Brief Encounter

Dear Uncle Clifford,

I work in the accounts department of Sludgethorpe Plastics, an organisation presumably well known to you because of its two Queen's Awards for Industry. Last month, during the firm's Christmas dance, I went outside for some fresh air.

In the car park I met this nice young man who had been taken unwell, assisted outside by two of his friends, and left propped against a lamp post.

Despite his obvious indisposition, he did not forget his manners and greeted me with a courteous, 'Hello, Doll. You and me could make sweet music together.' I thought that was ever so romantic. A bit like Humphrey Bogart in *Casablanca*.

We chatted for a while and then I assisted him back inside to the refreshment counter, where he bought me a packet of smoky bacon crisps and a Bacardi and lemonade with a cherry on the top and a little sunshade stuck in it.

He had a couple of pints of Guinness, which seemed to bring on his illness again, because he turned a peculiar shade of green and slid off the bar stool. Presumably a virus going about. Luckily, the evening was drawing to its close, and his two friends reappeared and carried him away to see him home safely.

What attracted me to him was his love of adventure and the open-air life. He is a dedicated angler, and from his accounts of titanic battles with ferocious and gigantic fish (man-eating gudgeon, I think he said, and piranha–bream hybrids), seemingly cast in the same heroic mould as Ernest Hemingway and Zane Grey.

He is a member of the Sludgethorpe Waltonians, a local angling club which apparently accepts only the most skilled and dedicated anglers as members, and whose achievements are the envy of the angling world.

I have hardly been able to sleep for thinking about him: the debonair way he pinched the end from his cigarette and placed the stub behind his right ear; his firm, manly grip around his glass of Guinness; the polite way he said 'Pardon' every time he burped.

Today I returned to work and despite looking high and low have been unable to trace him. All I know about him is that his name is Sidney.

What I want to know is:

(a) Am I being silly in wanting to renew our acquaintanceship?

(b) What could be the cause of his mysterious illness?

(c) Should I discover his whereabouts, what steps should I take?

Worried Blue Eyes

Dear Worried Blue Eyes,

(a) Silly? Not at all. Stupid, more like.

(b) From the symptoms you mention he was suffering from a state of toxicity brought about by excessive ingestion of a high-gravity alcoholic beverage. In non-medical terms, he was stonkers.

(c) What steps should you take? Long ones. In the opposite direction.

We're getting there . . .

This might be the Age of the Train, but travel by rail has its dangers for anglers. Certainly it was the cause of my arriving home wearing only one welly.

'Don't tell me,' said Dearly Beloved. 'It was all Mad Mac and Big McGinty's fault, plying you with drink.'

'If you are referring to the loss of my welly,' I said huffily, 'it had nothing to do with Mad Mac and Big McGinty. Nor with the Demon Drink. It was British Rail's fault.'

* * *

Asking around my stalwart comrades later, I heard some horrifying tales of mishaps to anglers on the permanent way. Dearly Beloved's suspicions were confirmed up to a point by the fact that those to whom the accidents had happened were all (with the exception of my own dear self) a little under the weather. But the other common denominator was the train.

These stories I shall now recount, having changed the names to protect the guilty.

Les was feeling decidedly queasy when he got on the train and, as it slowed down at the first stop, he stuck his head out of the window, for a health-giving chunder. As a consequence of which he lost his false teeth.

When the train stopped he opened the door, jumped down, walked back along the track, rescued his choppers and stuck them in his pocket. By which time the train had started to move again.

He grabbed at the nearest carriage, climbed up, but couldn't open the door. First Class passengers were treated to the horrific spectacle of a toothless Second Class drunk in a bobbly hat banging on the window of the moving train and screaming for aid and assistance.

A bit of swift communication-cord work saved the situation. Lucky Les got away with nothing more than a nasty

fright and having his name put in the British Rail Naughty Book.

* * *

Mad Mac has had several incidents on the train which have finally led him to travel by bus or to hitch a lift.

Apart from setting an old lady on fire, which had nothing to do with fishing and therefore has no place in this volume, at least two happenings are worthy of record.

The first was when the train started to move out of the station and the door to the compartment was opened by an angler festooned in tackle and gear. As the train gathered speed, the angler was flinging in his holdall and basket but obviously wasn't going to make it before he ran out of platform.

Mac sprang to his feet, grabbed the remaining gear and pulled it inside, then got hold of the bloke's collar and hauled him in just as the platform disappeared beneath him.

The angler collapsed in the opposite seat, lungs straining and covered in sweat.

'Thanks,' he said. 'You saved my life.'

'Think nothing of it,' said Mac, trembling all over and lighting a cigarette.

'Do you *mind*?' said the bloke. 'This is a non-smoker.'

. . . One of Mac's clubmates had a habit of getting very tired and emotional after every match. By the time they reached their local station he was never in any fit state even to collect his tackle, let alone get off the train. Although Mac did not know him very well, he took it upon himself every time to haul out both the bloke and the gear.

One Saturday night he stirred as Mac was hauling him off, and started to protest.

'Never mind that,' said Mac. 'Don't you understand? We're here. Come on, let's be having you.'

So saying, he dragged the bloke and his gear down on to the platform.

'There,' said Mac as the train pulled away. 'The last train, that was. Without me you'd still be on it.'

'I *wanted* to be,' wailed the bloke. 'I kept trying to tell you.

The wife's staying with her sister in Rugby – and I was supposed to carry on up there . . .'

*   *   *

There must be a special god who looks after drunks, otherwise Arthur would no longer be with us.

He'd stayed awake to be sure of not overshooting his stop, and finally he knew that the next station would be his.

When the train stopped, he picked up his gear and stepped out. Landing with a horrible crunch on the track.

He picked himself up, slung his gear back on the train, and climbed up after it.

'Silly me,' he announced to his fellow passengers. 'Wrong side.'

He opened the opposite door and stepped out – landing with a horrible crunch on the track.

Once again he climbed back on the train and looked desperately around for a third side to get out of.

'None of my business,' said one of the passengers. 'But there's a signal against us. We're still a quarter of a mile from the station . . .'

*   *   *

It was definitely a train which was responsible for the loss of my welly.

I'd arrived just as it was about to pull out, had slung my tackle on board, and was climbing on when my right welly slipped and jammed under the running-board.

The train started to move, so I jerked my welly free. Or at least I jerked my foot free. The welly stayed where it was, and then fell under the train. Presumably to be sliced into neat olive-green strips.

You feel such a fool. Arriving home wearing one olive-green welly and one white welly sock.

'It's my fault, really,' said Dearly Beloved as she opened the door to the one-wellied apparition on the step. 'I certainly can't say that my mother didn't warn me . . .'

An Act of Doc

'There's an insurance man in the paper,' I said to Dearly Beloved across the breakfast table, 'who reckons that the average husband is worth £500,000.'

'Really,' she said, looking at me in my morning glory. 'I'll take 50p for cash.'

Some people . . .

On the way to work, I read of a 15-year-old Italian lad, the world champion table-soccer player, whose right index finger – the one he flicks with – is insured for £25,000.

Gad, I thought, if a little lad's index finger is worth that much for just flicking some plastic footballers about, what must mine be worth? Where would I be without its aid on the bank for such essential operations as taking the ring off a can, guiding the hook into a pinkie and out of a perchie? Not to mention picking my nosie.

Shock, horror at the office. Phone call from Dave Bogart, hunky American person and former demon angler of Upper Black Eddy on the Delaware. Dave couldn't come to work on account of the fact that on his way home the night before he had fallen over a bloke who was cleaning his car in the dark. Broke both arms.

There was a lot of ribald speculation about what he was dialling with, but that's not the point. With both arms in plaster Dave would be in no condition for several weeks even to bait up, let alone cast out.

I'd better get insured, I thought, before something terrible happens to me. No use any longer relying on my lucky socks, rabbit's foot or Fozzie Bear mascot to keep me out of the emergency ward.

The trouble with angling, though, is that accidents are seldom straightforward, and it's rarely the likely one which gets you. Take my last boat trip out with Doc Thumper, ol' buddy mate and physician extraordinary.

Up the Thames we went, along the narrower upper reaches,

as is our wont. We came to a lock, the keeper of which was keeping an appointment with a pint somewhere.

'I'll operate the gates,' said Doc. 'And you can stay in charge of the boat.'

'Aye, aye, Cap'n,' I said. 'Have no fear. Old Long John Parker'll see 'ee roight. Oh, arrr . . .'

'On second thoughts,' said Doc. '*I'll* stay on board the boat. These things cost money. You work the gates. Sure you know how to do it?'

'Easy-peasy, Cap'n,' said I, leapt on the towpath, tied a rope around a bollard and winched open the first gate.

Fired with enthusiasm, I ran to the next set of gates and started winching madly away.

'Help!' cried Doc, as about 20 miles of Thames water started moving down towards him. 'You're supposed to close one gate before you open the other. And I'm supposed to be *inside* the lock!'

'What's keeping you?' I hollered, winching madly in reverse.

'Those twelve granny knots you tied around the bollard. Are you *sure* you've done this before?'

A little later it was Doc's turn to put us in peril of our young and blameless lives. Ahead was an island.

'There's a lovely little creek on the other side of that island,' said Doc. 'And I know an old lady who lives along there. She'll let us fish from the bottom of her garden.'

So saying, he swung the boat hard-a-starboard, or possibly port, round the back of the island. The current was flowing strongly in our favour.

'Soon be there,' said Doc. 'Oh, what's it say on that board sticking out of the water?'

'D-A-N-G-E-R. Danger,' I said. (As in Banger. My mind must have been on something else.) 'No! Ohmygawd! It's DANGER! As in Ranger!'

'As in what?' shouted Doc over the noise of the engine.

'Ranger! As in Lone Ranger! Tonto! Hi-yo Silver . . . away!'

'This is no time to be playing cowboys,' shouted Doc. 'Hell's bells! I completely forgot. There's a weir ahead.'

By a combination of skilful seamanship and pure fluke, Doc

turned the boat around and guided it painfully upstream out of the fast water. The old lady up the creek could wait for another day.

Farther downstream we approached a couple of small bays. 'This looks fine,' said Doc. 'We'll moor here.'

I crouched on the bows like a seasoned old salt, mooring rope in hand, and leapt onto the bank as we entered the first bay. The boat kept on going and dragged me halfway down the bank before I could let go of the rope and cling on to a handy tree.

'Why the hell didn't you stop?' I yelled.

'I meant the *second* bay,' said Doc. 'Stop messing about in that tree and make yourself useful.'

The useful bit was to moor the boat in the second bay. Doc threw up a couple of iron spikes which just missed my vitals, and a two-pound hammer which landed neatly on my foot.

'I'm getting a bit fed up with this,' I said.

'Not to worry,' said Doc. 'We're here now. Tell you what: while you're tackling up, I'll cook us a lovely mixed grill on the stove.'

* * *

Now do you see all the possibilities for accident on that one innocent trip out? The boat could have been turned over or washed away by the rush of lock water, or left dangling by the bows as the level dropped; it could have been swept over the weir; I would have had a ducking if it had not been for the handy tree; I just missed being speared by the mooring spikes; and was actually struck a deadly blow on the big toe by the two-pound hammer. Bang would have gone the no-claims bonus. But it wasn't any of those that did the damage.

That night, both Doc and I were assailed by fearsome indigestion and drove our respective spouses potty by groaning until the small hours. Now *that* was the real hazard of the trip, yet it probably wouldn't have been covered by insurance. It wasn't so much an Act of God as an Act of Doc.

You've never tried his cooking, have you?

Can Mother be wrong?

Dear Uncle Clifford,

Thank you ever so much for your advice last month about Sidney, the young man I met at the firm's Christmas dance. I'm sure it was very sound and given with the best of intentions, but I have bumped into him at work and I am afraid I have let my heart rule my head.

Sidney works in the packing department, parcelling up the plastic back scratchers and electronic commodes which are our firm's main export lines. It is a very highly skilled job calling for speed and a great deal of manual dexterity.

He did not return to work for a few days after the dance as a result of his indisposition, which he attributes to eating the prawn vol-au-vents prepared by the firm's canteen, but is now fit and well and without a trace of green upon his finely chiselled features.

He has taken me out once or twice to some very smart local nightspots – the *Bricklayer's Arms*, the *Weary Whippet* and the *Frenzied Ferret* – all of which have a very select clientele. He has introduced me to such culinary delights as scampi-flavoured pork scratchings and soup in the basket, and such sophisticated drinks as Tequila Sunrise, Harvey's Headbanger and Maiden's Regret.

His conversation is still as exciting and scintillating as when we first met. He's quite modest, really, but in moments of confidentiality he has told me how he landed a six-foot pike with his bare hands after his landing net broke under the weight, and how he gave the exhausted fish the kiss of life before returning it to the water.

The 60lb carp he landed from the Foundry Road Lock stretch of the canal was not only a personal best, but would have broken the British record had he entered it. He did not do so because he didn't want the canal to be overrun with glory hunters on ego trips, spoiling the fishing for himself and his fellow members. It is rare in these days of self-seeking and competitiveness to find someone so considerate and I think myself a really lucky girl.

My mother does not agree, however, and this is making me very unhappy. She was quite beside herself when I told her that Sidney was an angler.

'What *are* you thinking of, girl?' she said. 'Do you want a life of lonely weekends, burdened with decorating, lawn-mowing and bricklaying while he's off gallivanting along the canal? Do you want evenings of burnt meals because he's still not home from the boozer? Do you want the fridge full of maggots and the oven black from bread crusts which he was drying for groundbait and then forgot about? Do you want the carpets covered in mud and the living-room festooned with dripping keep nets? Do you want to find pike in the bath, rubby dubby in the sink, plates of rotten meat covered in bluebottles on the window-ledge?'

When I protested, she cut me short. 'I should know,' she said. 'I've been 25 years married to *that*.' Here she pointed to my father, who was snoring on the sofa after a hard evening's committee work down at his own angling club, the Slagville Piscatorials. Committee work must be very strenuous, because Father always returns with his eyes a little out of focus, a stumbling walk indicative of total exhaustion, and invariably collapses on the sofa once he's had his tea.

Please tell me my mother's wrong, Uncle Clifford. That life with an angler isn't as bad as she's painted it.

Worried Blue Eyes

Dear Worried Blue Eyes,

Yes, my dear, your mother's wrong.
Life with an angler isn't always as bad as she's painted it.
Often it's a damn sight worse.

Lost and found

Lovely story in the papers about a little lad from Wigan whose bike was stolen, along with his sister's. Fishing next day, by pure accident, he reeled in both bikes from the claypit where they had been dumped.

Warms the old cockles, a story like that. I noticed it particularly because I was on the trail of lost-and-found stories after coming across a lone welly in the middle of a field.

In good condition, in fact hardly worn, the welly was standing upright and pointing away from the river.

What was its sinister secret? Had the angler been surprised by a bull which had snuck up behind him and tossed him out of the welly? Or had he leapt out of it in sheer fright? Worse, had he been rude to the old lady selling lucky white heather and been turned into a toad?

As the welly was pointing away from the water, had he perhaps been fleeing the wrath of his fellow anglers after being caught fiddling a match? Or was it the appearance of Ken Kong, the Banzai Bailiff, which had caused him to leave so precipitately?

On the other hand, perhaps there was nothing sinister about it at all. Perhaps it had been cast aside by a one-legged angler who had a sudden urge to hop barefoot through the grass. You know how it takes people sometimes, especially towards the full moon.

All of a sudden, the lost-and-found stories started coming thick and fast. There was the Essex couple who went fishing on the Norfolk Broads. The wife caught an old shoe. For a joke, the husband took it home and put it in a glass case. When his sister-in-law saw it she yelled, 'My shoe!' It was one she'd lost on holiday on the Broads six weeks earlier.

Then there was the American fisherman who lost his false teeth in a lake 80 feet deep. A week later he caught a 20lb catfish. Inside the catfish were his false teeth. A quick scrub under the tap and they were as good as new.

One story which crops up every year, and which is always presented as the gospel truth, is about the two anglers out sea fishing. One is sick over the side and loses his false teeth. The other bloke, for a laugh, attaches his own false teeth to his line and pretends to catch them. He gives them to his mate who tries them out, finds they don't fit . . . and chucks them over the side.

* * *

I was beachfishing once when a distressed lady person came along, looking for her engagement ring. There didn't seem to be much chance of finding it, as she'd been walking along the sea's edge and the tide was coming in. But suddenly there was a twinkle as a wave came and went – and there was the ring on the sand.

A couple of days later at the same spot, I found I'd lost a fiver. *Nil desperandum*, I thought. Do what the lady person did and retrace your steps. I did, and was rewarded with the Luck of the Parkers. There wasn't a sign of the flaming thing.

One jolly jape which is always good for a laugh at the club is to go in and ask, 'Anybody here lost a hundred quid boron rod and a bent old rod rest?'

There's always one bloke who says, 'Yes – me.'

'You're in luck,' you say. 'I've found the bent old rod rest.'

This gets two laughs. The first at the bloke's embarrassment and discomfiture. The second at the sight of you getting the rod rest knotted around your neck. (Why are the blokes who fall for the joke always seven-foot-three and of a nasty disposition?)

I overheard a lost-and-found operation story the other day. A lady person with dreadful sinus trouble. Had it for years. She went into hospital to have it seen to, and the surgeon extracted a tiddlywink which she'd pushed up her nose 20-odd years before as a child. A yellow one, it was. Just shows the danger of absent-mindedness. Or of tiddling instead of winking.

It put me in mind of the angler who rang up the hospital from a phone box by the water.

'My little lad's swallowed a four-inch pike spoon,' he said. 'Trebles and all.'

'Don't panic,' said the hospital. 'We'll be round right away. What are you doing meantime?'

'Legering. What else?'

Where's there's a will

The other week I had to see the bank manager about some trifling deficiency in my account.

After listening in bored disbelief to my fibs, and giving me the statutory time for ritual grovelling, he asked: 'Have you made a will?'

Gad, I thought. Do I look as bad as that?

The same evening the insurance man dropped in to collect his premiums and drum up some more business.

After explaining how infinitely more I was worth dead than alive, he said, 'And of course the money goes immediately to your beneficiaries. No need to hang around waiting for probate on your will.'

'I'm getting worried,' I said to Dearly Beloved after he'd gone. 'That's the second time today somebody's mentioned my will.'

'Take no notice, love,' she said. 'But I'd get it done soon all the same. You *are* looking a bit frayed round the edges.'

Et tu, Petal?

I called round at Doc Thumper's in a state of foreboding and tremblement, and asked him to give me a National Health once-over.

'Don't fret,' he said when he'd finished. 'If you give up smoking and drinking and impure thoughts, you could last for weeks. Oh, and could you put me down for your river rod? I've always fancied that.'

Really, I'm in as good nick as a man of my age and habits can expect to be (i.e. only semi-decrepit). But it comes to us all in the end, as Izaak Walton observed when he sat on his rod rest, so I'd better put my affairs in order. Here goes, then:

LAST WILL AND TESTAMENT

I, Clifford John Parker, being of sound mind or thereabouts, do hereby give and bequeath:

To my bank manager, Mr Adolf Facegrind: my overdraft.

To Doc Thumper: my river rod. You will find out soon enough that there's an incurable set in the top joint, that two of the rings need urgent re-whipping, and that there's a hole in the bottom of the case where the mice got at it.

To Big McGinty: my wicker basket. You may as well have it, as it's been fit for nowt since you sat on it. Before you sit on it again I would suggest that you have the legs trued up from their present angle of 30 degrees to the vertical, have the splintered wickerwork re-wickered, and a heavy-duty steel joist inserted under the lid.

To Mad Mac: the last dregs of Dr Dumdum's Electric Wonder Oil as an insurance against your no longer being able to find the little Indian with a turban in the pub who sold it to you in bulk all those years ago. Please use it only as a groundbait additive and do not advise people to rub their chests with it as a specific against whatever ails them. Compounded as it is of seal oil and sulphuric acid, it makes the wearer smell like an old kipper. All it did for me as an unguent was to get me bitten by Daft Cat.

To Daft Cat: the bottle of pilchard oil in the shed. This is to be used to boost the pussycat appeal of the expensive tins of pet food at which you repeatedly turn up your nose.

To the Victoria and Albert Museum (Historical Costume Department): my Man United bobbly hat, anorak, pully, trousers, lucky socks and wellies. This unique collection of authentic angling clobber will leave future generations in no doubt about what the typical 20th-century coarse fisherman looked like. If you are willing not to have the lot fumigated, it will give them also some idea of what the typical 20th-century coarse fisherman smelled like.

To my club secretary, Mr Sid Borgia: a couple of stones from the bank of the Grand Union Canal. See how much blood you can get out of *them*.

To Mr Fritz Lowzitrowsers, the match steward who disqualified me last season for coughing: two fingers.

[Ee . . . I'm enjoying this.]

To my dear mother-in-law: the large tin of weedkiller in the greenhouse. One tablespoon to be taken three times a day. Neat.

To – Ouch! What, Petal? Of *course* I didn't mean it about your mother. One of the nicest little – Oof! Gerroff!

* * *

'Sorry, Pet. I got carried away.'

'Another crack like that about my mother and you will be – in a pine box.'

Perhaps it's as well I made a will after all . . .

Just an idea

Cousin Jim from Leeds lent me a lovely old book, published in 1940 and edited by E. Marshall-Hardy, entitled *Anglers' Ideas*.

'Nice of you, Jim lad,' I said. 'You want my professional opinion on the ideas, eh?'

'No,' he said. 'I've been watching you fish and I thought you could use a few.'

'Me too,' said young Laura, daughter of Jim. 'I think me Uncle Clifford's crackers.'

Very bright is our Laura. And deserving of a serious and considered reply. A touch of the child psychology.

'Belt up, Shorthouse,' I said. 'Who asked you?'

* * *

It's been interesting to go through the ideas, many of which have stood the test of time. Others must have died the death yonks ago.

There's a tip, for instance, on keeping your feet warm in winter: 'Procure a rabbit skin or two from the fishmonger,' says the contributor. (Those were the days. Rabbits from the fishmonger. And with the fur still on.)

What you do is to peg out the skin on a board, fur side down, and rub threepennyworth of saltpetre and alum into the skin. (In those days you were able to buy saltpetre without a visit from the bomb squad.) Leave the skin for a fortnight, then cut out two bits to fit inside your wellies, fur side up.

Easy-peasy. But from what I remember from my own skin-curing days (I was into Davy Crockett hats at the time), it's difficult to get the skin to go soft. Not much use having lovely warm feet if you can't hobble as far as the water because of the corrugated bunny hide in your wellies.

'Chew it,' said Mad Mac. 'Like the American Indian and Eskimo women used to do. You've seen them in the old photographs.'

'It may have escaped your notice, ol' buddy,' I said, 'that

the women in those photographs had one thing in common. Not a tooth between the lot of 'em.'

It is difficult to get a skin cured by an amateur to stay cured. One reason I am not a Davy Crockett hat millionaire was that after a week the skin used to pong something awful. A couple of trips with an angler's foot in the close confines of a welly would be as much as the average home-cured fun fur could stand before cheese mite set in.

* * *

One tip which has survived well is tying such droppable things as disgorgers and keys onto a cork, so that if they're dropped into the water they can be rescued. Doc Thumper was using this one on his last boat trip.

'See,' he said, before we boarded, dropping the key to the boat into the Upper Thames. 'I can now just pick it – Oops!'

One thing you have to allow for on the Upper Thames is the current. It helps to have a landing net already made up. After a couple of minutes of panic the key was netted and Doc proudly inserted it into the cabin door. Or he would have done if it had not refused to go.

There it was. A key guaranteed to float. Never to disappear from sight into the weedy depths. Unsinkable. Unlosable.

Just a pity it was the wrong key.

* * *

A non-skid device for muddy river banks consists of a pair of metal plates, each with four-inch nails riveted in, which can be strapped to your boots. It looks very effective – but *four-inch* nails? How many anglers must have been stuck there all night, stapled to the bank by four-inch nails, before the designer decided that perhaps half-inch galvanised clout nails would be enough? And how many anglers broke a leg or two trying to stilt-walk across a stretch of hard bank?

* * *

A then new idea for stocking remote lakes in Canada was dropping trout from the air. Professor Gustave of Montreal

University had made experiments which included dropping a four-pound trout into a lake from 1,000 feet. It was recovered alive for observation. Professor Gustave then presumably made his name with a paper on 'The Effects of Air Sickness, Free Fall, Deceleration and Concussion on Four-Pound Trout'.

But what was happening to anglers on remote Canadian lakes while all this was going on? What if the trout-dropper's aim was off? What if the wind changed?

'It was like this, Doc. I was sitting on the bank when all of a sudden it started raining fish. This big trout fell from the sky and hit me on the –'

'Of course, of course. Now put on this canvas jacket and relax. I'll just tie these tapes at the back and have you wheeled into this luxury consulting room. Like it? All those beautiful padded walls . . .'

* * *

Worms can be given a good colour, apparently, by mixing brick-dust with the scouring moss. Early reports from the Parker Laboratory (tel: Transylvania Six-Five-Thousand) indicate that the colour is slow in coming but that constipation is quick in setting in. Hard on the worms, but it might be the answer to a quick-sinking bait for weightless casting.

Turn your worms white overnight, it says here, by sticking them in a jar of milk topped off by a layer of moss. This I have just done. For results, see Stop Press.

* * *

To keep moths out of your flies, says another contributor, sprinkle them with white pepper. As one who has never been troubled with moths in his flies, and who would be afeard of peppering them for all sorts of reasons, all I can do is pass this on.

* * *

To prevent insect bites you mix seven parts of glycerine with one of turpentine and apply it to the eyebrows and the back of the ears. This I am disinclined to believe on account of being

31

bitten by insects everywhere but on the eyebrows and the back of the ears.

The only real answer, as I have mentioned here and in previous volumes, is Dr Dumdum's Electric Wonder Oil, bought in bulk by Mad Mac from a little Indian with a turban in a pub in Hemel Hempstead. It is a mixture of seal oil and sulphuric acid, which you splash all over and which makes you smell like an old kipper. This keeps away almost every living creature, including the wife.

The one exception is the cat, who bites a chunk out of your leg as soon as you step inside the door.

To get rid of a cat who bites a chunk out of your leg as soon as you step inside the door, take one two-pound hammer ...

STOP PRESS
PARKER LAB REPORTS FINE JAR OF CREAM CHEESE. WORMS FETCHINGLY PALE BUT REGRETTABLY NON-FUNCTIONAL (I.E. DEAD). MOSS NEVER LOOKED BETTER.

Is there another?

Dear Uncle Clifford,

Something has gone terribly wrong with my relationship with Sidney. It is now March 14th and I have hardly seen him all month.

I have tackled him at work about it, but he doesn't seem to hear. All he can say, with a faraway look in his eye, is, 'I'll explain some time, Doll, but don't bother me now. I've too many things on my mind. Time's running out.'

Time's running out. That's the bit that worries me. I do hope he hasn't contracted some terminal illness which he is keeping from me to spare my feelings. I know he has occasional trouble with dandruff and athlete's foot, but the medical dictionary at the local library does not mention any likelihood of fatality.

Perhaps his recent bereavements are preying on his mind. During the first week of the month he had a day off work to attend his grandmother's funeral. During the second week he had another day off to attend his other grandmother's funeral.

There was some trouble when the personnel manager pointed out that Sidney had two days off last year, at the same time, to attend the funerals of both his grandmothers. But, as Sidney pointed out, was it his fault if both his grandfathers had got married again? To elderly ladies in indifferent health?

At a time like this I don't think the personnel manager should harass the poor lamb. Some people have no sensitivity at all.

I have never seen much of Sidney at weekends, but this I accept. As he points out so eloquently, 'A man's got to do what a man's got to do.' (He sounds ever so much like John Wayne when he says that.) But for the past fortnight I have seen nothing of him in the evenings, either. As soon as the buzzer goes for knocking-off time, he's out of the packing department and away. Sometimes he goes even earlier, leaving a whole benchful of back scratchers and commodes to be packed the following morning. And often he's late in for work, looking pale and bleary eyed, as if he's had little or no sleep.

Has he gone off me? I ask myself. Has his passion cooled? His ardour subsided? Has he contracted some secret vice such as gambling, fretwork or bingo which is claiming his time in the evenings? Worse – in fact the unthinkable – has he got another woman?

Worried Blue Eyes

Dear Worried Blue Eyes,

Calm down. Put your mind at rest. Behaviour such as Sidney's is quite normal among coarse fishermen at this time of year. The season ended on March 14, the day you wrote your letter. I'll lay odds-on that you've seen plenty of him since and that the romantic aspect of your relationship, which may seem to have been in the doldrums for at least a couple of weeks, has blossomed into something quite torrid and tempestuous.

Time *was* running out for Sidney, time to squeeze in the last remaining hours of fishing before the final whistle. He'll have been at it morning and evening, and possibly all through the night. Not only would he not have time for another woman, he wouldn't even have the strength.

Don't grieve too much for the dead grandmothers. At this time of year in angling circles there is an abnormally high death rate among grandmas, with an equally abnormal number of funerals to attend. Those anglers who have run out of grandmas have to rely on annual epidemics of bad backs, varicose veins and chronic piles.

Stuffing, anyone?

Taxidermy, as you know, comes from the Greek *taxis* (an arranging) and *derma* (skin). Webster's Dictionary goes on to define it as: 'The art of treating, stuffing and mounting the skins of animals so that they retain their natural appearance.'

Natural appearance is no good to the likes of me. What the Parker Academy of Alternative Stuffing for the Piscatorially Underprivileged has been working on is the twelve-inch gudgeon, the two-foot perch and the eight-foot pike. From originals of four, six and twelve inches respectively. These being the usual lengths for anybody as piscatorially underprivileged as I am.

Scoff ye not. Setting up a big fish is skilful enough. Setting up a little 'un, especially if it has to finish up several times its original size, takes something extra, something special: dishonesty.

Be fair: stretching a fish you've caught yourself is perhaps less dishonest than buying a stuffed fish caught by somebody else. I did think once of parting with a few bob for a decent-sized stuffed pike, caught by somebody better at it.

'Not exactly the one I caught,' I could say. 'But uncommonly like it. Especially around the eyes.'

(Stranger things have happened. Guayaquil City Council, in Ecuador, wanted to put up a statue to José Olmedo, a local lad who'd become a great poet. They couldn't raise the ready, so they bought a secondhand statue of Lord Byron and put José's name on it. Nobody complained.)

How do we get this something extra? You could always use three fish instead of one and stick extra panels into the body. But not only is this *really* cheating, it's easily detectable, which is worse. Pike, for instance, have 'thumbprints' along their sides, the pattern of which is unique to each fish. A sudden change of thumbprints halfway along indicates that the original pike has got company.

If we're going to be dishonest, at least let's be honest about

35

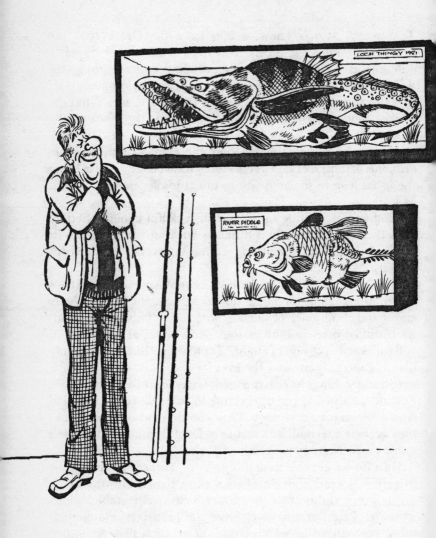

it. One fish at a time. It's surprising what you can do to the length of even a tiddler by the judicious application of the garden roller. It can be done with less effort by leaving the fish in the road and waiting for the next juggernaut, but then it needs a lot of ironing to get the tyre marks out.

You can place it between two layers of newspaper and stick it in a trouser press. But as few anglers own a trouser press – to judge by the look of them anyway – that's probably a daft suggestion. An alternative is to stick the fish underneath the mattress for a couple of weeks, though the Marriage Guidance Council is understood to disapprove of the practice.

Instead of packing it with sand to dry out, try using brewer's yeast. Put it in a moderate oven and stand well back.

You can stretch the skin over a ready-made supersize plaster cast. I saw a telly programme which showed an American taxidermist at work. He was setting up the skin of a little squirrel which some juvenile sadist had shot.

Out of a drawer came a plaster model of a hairless giant squirrel. Over went the skin. A few discreet tugs – and there was the biggest and most muscular squirrel known to man.

As well as size, you can give the fish something extra in the way of ferocity. When you're choosing the glass eyes, go for something crazed and bloodshot. Have the top lip curled back in a snarl. And stick in the odd fang or two. A set of Dracula choppers from the local joke shop looks very effective:

'Yerss . . . That gudgeon there sank its teeth into the toe of me welly and *wouldn't* let go. It took three blokes to prise the thing loose. Even then it had the backside out of the pants of one of them. Not surprising with those teeth. Here's the welly in the next case. See the holes . . .?'

* * *

Finally, a touching and (so I'm told) true taxidermy story. An old lady had a pet duck for years, then the poor old thing died. (The duck, not the lady.)

Heartbroken, she packed it off to a big department store which had a taxidermy service. But she didn't specify which department and simply enclosed a note saying, 'Please stuff my duck.'

It came back within a couple of days. Without a feather on it. Stuffed with sage and onion.

A little thing entitled . . .

It's not fair. Sports such as soccer and rugby have their own collections of songs and Neanderthal-type chants (*Oggi-Oggi-Oggi!* and all that stuff), while angling's outward lyrical expression is confined to a few corny jokes about telling fibs and falling in the water.

I'm doing something about it, on a highly refined plane, by producing a collection of songs for swinging anglers and rumbustious rhymes for all occasions. Entitled *The Parker Anthology of Angling Songs and Stirring Recitations*, it's coming along quite well.

A masterwork such as this cannot be rushed, but I thought you'd like to hear how it is getting on. I tend to get stuck after the first verse, so you might like to finish off a few songs for yourself.

I started, as I often do, by responding to the Call of the Sea. This little poem is guaranteed to stir the corpuscles of every red-blooded Englishman:

> *I must go down to Blackpool again,*
> *To the lonely sea and sky.*
> *Tea on the sands and fish and chips,*
> *Or mushy peas and a pie.*

Poor old Morecambe, Blackpool's neighbour, comes in for a lot of stick. ('An H-bomb was dropped on Morecambe last night. Fifteen pounds' worth of damage was done.') Last year I decided to see for myself and went on the ten-minute Grand Tour. Las Vegas need have no fear. (Tune: *Sloop John B.*):

> *We've come from the Sloop John B.,*
> *My grandfather and me.*
> *Around Morecambe town we did roam.*
> *We didn't half tut,*
> *'Cos Morecambe was shut,*

> *So we raved up in Rochdale*
> *And then we went home.*

There's an old nautical poem which is always difficult to render acceptable in polite company, but I think I'm on the way:

> *'Twas on the Good Ship Venus,*
> *By gad, you should have seen us.*

(Hang on a minute, you lot. Hang on.)

> *The skipper, old Ted, was out of his head*
> *On one of his regular beanos.*

If anybody can supply a second verse without getting locked up, he's a better man than I am.

A bone of contention every year is the two-fish limit imposed on some charter boats. Which means that however many fish an angler catches, he can only take away two, the remainder being sold by the skipper. This can cause the occasional fracas between the skipper and the lads who hadn't read the small print. There's nothing wrong with the two-fish limit so long as you do read the small print and the price is right, but some skippers have a reputation for making the lads work hard for the privilege of standing on their decks. No messing about enjoying yourself: you're there to *fish*. (Tune: *Johnny Come Down to Hilo*):

> *I nebber seen de like*
> *Since I bin born*
> *Of a two-fish skipper*
> *Wid his sea boots on,*
> *Singin' 'Johnny, get off dat Li-lo!'*
> *Poor old man . . .*

A quick change of tempo, but still on the same tack. (Tune: *Old Man River*):

Anglers all work for de two-fish skipper.
Anglers all work while de skipper say,
'Keep castin' dem baits from de dawn 'til sunset,
'Pumpin' dem fish 'til de Judgment Day.'

Don' look up
An' don' look down.
Don' dare make dat skipper frown.
Pump dat fish.
Put down dat rum.
Yo' ain't got time
To scratch yo' bu-hum . . .

Whatever boat you fish from, however calm the weather, you eventually hit open water. Which has a nasty habit of going up and down. And which sorts out the men from the boys. (Tune: *One Friday Morn*):

Three times round went our gallant ship
And three times round went she.
Three times our breakfasses* went up
*   and up aloft,*
Then they sank to the bottom of the sea,
*   the sea, the sea.*
Then they sank to the bottom of the sea.

Back to gentler waters, and warmer ones – like the canal near St Helens in Lancashire where a warm-water outfall for several years supported a healthy colony of tropical fish, dumped there by petshop owners with cash-flow problems. (Tune: *Banana Boat Song*):

---

* (a) It has to be *breakfasses* to make it scan.
  (b) That's how they say it where I come from.

> *Hey, Mister Tallyman,*
> *Tally me piranha.*
> *It's bit me thumb*
> *An' I wanna go home . . .*

That song has a particular appeal to nightfishers. Especially nightfishers whose sensory deprivation has led to some illusion about the size of the catch:

> *Five-foot, six-foot, seven-foot pike!*
> *Daylight come an' I wanna go home.*
> *Never get the flaming thing on me bike!*
> *Daylight come an' I wanna go home . . .*

There is a high incidence of domestic friction in angling families. It is caused mainly by wives who do not understand why their Ever-Lovings arrive home at three in the morning, a bit tired and emotional and falling about, and then have to get up at five to start the whole thing all over again. The poor lad in the next song has arrived on the bank after having been through just such a misunderstanding. (Tune: *John Peel*):

> *D'ye ken old Fred*
> *With his nose so red,*
> *And a lump on his head*
> *Where he fell out of bed?*
> *His wife was uptight*
> *So she gave him one last night,*
> *And another just for luck*
> *In the morning . . .*

There's nothing like an old fashioned dramatic monologue, I always say. I always say it when I run out of anything sensible to contribute. This one, based on *The Green Eye of the Little Yellow God*, is a swine to finish. Anyway, try the first verse for starters:

There's a cack-handed, cross-eyed angler
To the north of Wigan Pier,
Hooking the bloke sitting next to him,
Then saying, 'What's this ear?'

Thank you, members of the Vincent Van Gogh Appreciation Society. And if you can do any better . . .

Sidney turns torrid

Dear Uncle Clifford,

Bless you. You were so right about my Sidney. Since March 15th he has confessed all. How he was spending every minute of his spare time down at the canal. How his abstracted manner was caused by the knowledge that he had only a little time to catch another potential record breaker. How his grandmothers' funerals were little white lies, necessary fabrications to get another two precious days' fishing in.

Sidney is not a vain man, but he does pride himself upon his physical fitness and thought it would not do for him to be absent with a bad back, varicose veins or chronic piles.

The romantic side of our relationship took some time to blossom again. For the first fortnight of the close season, Sidney was very down, given to long solitary walks by the canal and brooding over his Guinness on our evenings out.

'Three months,' he kept muttering. 'Three bloody months! What the hell do fish need three months for? It's not as if their sex life is anything to write home about. Five minutes and it's all over. And that's for a whole bloody year . . .'

It's not like my Sidney to use language like that in front of me, so he must have been very upset indeed.

It cheered him up to show me the photographs of his specimen catches during the season past. I must admit that they didn't look all that big to me, but Sidney explained that was because of the optical illusions created by the camera. Just as people look bigger and fatter on the television screen, so fish look smaller in still photographs. You have to see fish in the round, Sidney says, to appreciate fully their length and bulk, not to mention their fighting qualities.

At the end of the month he took me to the Sludgethorpe Waltonians' annual dinner and prizegiving. It started off quite well, even though some of the speeches were a bit boring and others were a bit near the knuckle. When the chairman recited several variations on 'She was only a fisherman's daughter', I didn't know where to put my face.

The prizegiving itself was a bit disappointing. My Sidney got only one prize, the Cack-hander of the Year award, which I think must be for some special angling skill. It was obviously a very popular award, judging from the applause and cheers as Sidney collected his prize, but he didn't seem too pleased about it. Well, not judging by the gestures he was making to the awards committee members.

The evening came to a sad conclusion, owing to some little disagreement between Sidney and the awards committee chairman. This resulted in their stepping outside to discuss the matter further.

When they returned, Sidney had a split lip and the beginnings of a black eye. He had walked into something in the dark, he said. The chairman of the awards committee must have done the same, as he came back shaking his right hand and blowing on his knuckles.

Why I'm writing now is that finally our romance has blossomed, as you said it would, into something torrid and tempestuous. I'm worried that it's a bit too torrid and tempestuous.

With all the time on his hands now, and the obvious frustration of not being able to pursue his beloved sport, Sidney has turned into a real hot-blooded Latin lover. He makes passionate love to me whenever the mood takes him, and with no regard for time or place. The last time it happened was in the *Frenzied Ferret* on the pool table. That wouldn't have been so bad if the place hadn't been so crowded and there hadn't been a game in progress. What *can* I do? (In haste. Here comes Sidney again.)

Worried Blue Eyes

P.S.: Excuse wobbly writing.

Dear Worried Blue Eyes,

See if he'll take up trout fishing or try to get him interested in some close-season activity, such as building a wormarium or repairing his tackle. Otherwise there's not a lot you can do, apart from chucking a bucket of cold water over him. Meantime, change your pub. Or at least ask him to wait until the pool game's over.

For whom the bells toll

Marriage tends to take the angler unawares, mainly because the womenfolk organise it while he's trying to concentrate on something else.

There he is on the bank, with his beloved sitting behind him. She's wittering on. He's trying to keep his eyes on the float and give her sensible answers at the same time.

'What, love? The guests? Just a minute. Auntie Ida? Yeah. Uncle Cedric with the wooden leg and bald head? Yeah, I know the one. Looks like a toffee apple. Hey up – I've got a nibble.

'Bridesmaids? Hang on – hell, it dipped then. I wish you wouldn't keep nattering at times like this. What *about* bridesmaids? What for? Wedding? Whose wedding? *Our* wedding? Aaarrrgh!'

* * *

For what it's worth, and in the hope of killing some of the pain, here comes Uncle Clifford's advice to young lads for whom there is No Way Out.

Ideally, fix the date for the close season. This is not always possible, on account of the heavy demand. Sometimes, too, the prospective father-in-law is not prepared to wait until the next close season and emphasises the point by investing in a large-bore shotgun.

So what do you do about an in-season wedding? First, accept that it is the bride's day. Keep it clear of matches in the afternoon – an afternoon match only makes you twitchy during the reception, wondering whether you can get away in time to draw a peg. And certainly cancel the nightfishing trip.

If you can't fix the wedding for mid-week, Saturday's the next best bet. At least it gives you Sunday clear.

The choice of Best Man is crucial. He's responsible for the smooth running of the whole thing and therefore has to be organised, intelligent, tactful and sober.

So don't pick your mate. How many anglers have a mate who is organised, intelligent, tactful and sober? And how many mates, faced with a trembling, ashen-faced groom, have the heart to frogmarch him to the church when he's pleading to be smuggled to the nearest Foreign Legion recruiting centre?

Hire your Best Man from a security agency. A seventeen-stone Best Man from Rent-A-Heavy not only makes sure the proceedings go according to plan, but also comes in very handy when the fracas breaks out at the reception.

I'm afraid that fracas tend to break out at anglers' weddings more often than at normal ones.

For a start, the bride's mother is seldom keen on her Little Girl marrying an angler. Especially if she's married to one herself. She is pre-disposed to display attitudes of disapproval which mothers-in-law normally keep in check until at least after the honeymoon.

For a second, the angler's mates are there under protest. They're missing their morning's fishing and are inclined to compensate by hitting the grog rather early.

It is not unknown for those with a match in the afternoon to turn up in their wellies and stack their tackle in the vestry. (See *Mad Mac and Other Animals: Vol IV.*) This leads to complaints from the bride's mother and defiant replications from the lads. Before the vicar has finished saying his piece, an Atmosphere has set in.

By the time the reception is under way, the Atmosphere has intensified to the point of open hostility. And when the bride's mother catches one of the lads nicking chunks of wedding-cake for his groundbait, the marzipan really hits the fan.

The problem is exacerbated (by gum, that's better out than in) when the bride's and groom's families belong to rival angling clubs. There is no way that the old feuds can be kept under wraps for the whole of the reception. The Best Man's first anti-fracas duty is usually to separate the two fathers-in-law who are knocking hell out of one another under the table during the toast to The Happy Couple.

Another important duty for the Best Man is to ensure the security of the couple's honeymoon luggage and the absolute secrecy of their destination. Anglers' mates think it ever such a jolly jape to fill vanity cases with maggies or ripe squid, and to slip long-dead pike between the covers of the nuptial couch.

Anglers' brides tend not to see the joke. They're funny that way.

Raising the tone

'Caught these myself,' said Tactful Tetters, holding up a brace of lovely trout.

'You never did,' I said.

'I did so,' said Tetters, looking all peeved.

'Then why have you just taken them out of a bag marked *Sid Marbles, High Class Fishmonger and Purveyor of Piscatorial Products to the Gentry*?'

'Because that's where I caught them. In Sid's High Class Emporium. In this very bag. I opened the bag and Sid threw the trout across the counter. Now who's fibbing?'

Tetters is by no means a snob. You can tell that by the company he keeps. But the trout did go to his head a bit.

'Having these for my tea,' he said.

'What with?' I asked, bracing myself for an in-depth culinary discussion. 'Chips?'

'Don't be so common,' said Tetters. '*Pommes frites*, I'm having. *Truite à la Meunière et Pommes Frites à la Tetters. Avec* . . . Er . . . *Avec* . . .'

'*Avec* what?'

'Dunno,' he said. 'What's the French for Mushy Peas?'

* * *

I shudder to think what will happen to Tetters if the salmon return to the Thames and its tributaries in catchable numbers. Worse, if they ever make the Grand Union Canal. Should Tetters accidentally catch one in there, he'll be completely unbearable. I can see the menu now:

Saumon Fumé
et
Pommes Frites à la Tetters
avec
Mushy Peas Anglaises à la Sludgethorpe

Talking about Sludgethorpe, what's going to happen to all the Sludgethorpe Waltonians – all the happy, unpretentious little angling clubs – if the salmon do come back in numbers?

Even if the filthy rich don't move in and take over the waters, the switch from gudgeon to salmon would be bound to have a dramatic effect. Especially if the women get to hear about it.

'Yerss ... My Albert caught a salmon near Foundry Road Lock only last week. Four whole pounds it weighed. Not so big as the one Prince Charles caught on the Spey, but then my Albert didn't have a goolie to help him ...'

And what's going to happen at the clubhouse when the tone is raised?

Net curtains at the windows. Perhaps even glass in the windows instead of the bits of cardboard as at present. Wellies to be left at the door.

The subs would go up to pay for the improvements. Annual Full Membership £3,500. Associate Membership £2,500. Juniors and Pensioners £1,250.

Social nights will never be the same once we start receiving invitations which read:

> Mrs and Mrs Albert Higginbottom
> are cordially invited to the
> Sludgethorpe Waltonians'
> Annual Hotpot Supper
>
> 7.30 p.m. for 8 p.m.
> Carriages at 11 p.m.
>
> To be held at the Balmoral Suite
> Foundry Road Clubhouse
> Wednesday 7th April 1988
> Dress Formal
> Decorations and teeth to be worn
>
> R.S.V.P.
> Sir Fred Chuckerbutty
> Social Secretary

N.B. The Committee will expect members and guests to observe a modicum of decorum as laid down in the Regulations, i.e.: No swearing, spitting, fisticuffs, falling about or purloining of pie crusts for groundbait.

* * *

It could be even worse. The Hotpot Suppers could disappear altogether, to be replaced by Smoked Salmon Evenings, with vol-au-vents and daft things on sticks.

We could be expected to sup our pints with our little fingers sticking out to show our breeding. ('No blowing off of froth, old chap. And would you mind removing your cap in the Mess?')

While we're thinking the Unthinkable, what if draught bitter is banned as being *infra dig* and replaced by champagne? Which, as every serious beer drinker knows, is vastly overrated.

There have been claims recently that the Thames has not been cleaned up as much as was originally thought; that the return of the salmon could have been something of a fluke.

It pains me to say it, but let's hope so. Otherwise it could be the End of Fishing and Supping as We Know It.

The bodies in question

'Oops, sorry ducks,' said Dozy Doris, the new barmaid. 'I've dropped your change in your pint.'

I had already gathered that from the splash which soaked my new woolly tie, bought by Dearly Beloved to keep my little chest warm on the bank.

'Never mind, love,' I said. 'I can't wait twenty minutes for you to pull another pint. I'll sup this before you do any more damage and I'll fish the change out afterwards.'

Of course I forgot, and with the last swig a 1p piece went down the wrong way. As I staggered about coughing, spluttering and turning blue, Big McGinty clouted me on the back. The 1p piece shot out and hit the dartboard, scoring the only double top I'd made all year.

It would have made a better story if I'd swallowed it. Then I could have done the bit about ringing Doc Thumper:

'I've swallowed a coin, Doc. What shall I do?'

'Don't worry. Leave it till morning and see if there's any change.'

But it brought to mind the story about the lad on the bank who was fixing weights on the line with his teeth and swallowed a couple of them. When he got home he hiccupped twice and shot the cat.

It reminded me, too, that every season sees another bumper crop of anglers' ailments. Among the good old good ones like Basket Bum, Reservoir Ears and Nightfisher's nose, there are always some hitherto unknown to medical science.

Take *Duck Pimples*, for instance, brought on by exposure on windswept reservoirs. At one time anglers used to suffer from goose pimples. But these days, with the ever rising cost of bait, tackle and tickets, duck pimples are all we can afford.

Fumbler's Finger is especially prevalent in the cold weather, when hands are stiff and numb. The finger is the one the angler takes into the surgery stuck up in the air. Diagnosis is not difficult: it's either full of hooks or it's got a pike clenched firmly on the end of it.

* * *

Matchmen are particularly prone to ailments.

Match Winner's Elbow is to fishing what Tennis Elbow is to tennis. (Gad, the cutting-through mind of this lad. He explains everything so clearly.) It's a swelling of the right elbow joint caused by the constant flexing of the tiddler snatcher.

Match Loser's Elbow is an outbreak of corns on the joint of the left arm, caused by leaning on the bar: either before the match during dreams of the glories to come, or after the match during remorse about the glories which didn't.

Match Winner's Back is black and blue as a result of being slapped so heartily by his stalwart comrades. Not so much in congratulation as in the hope that he'll buy pints all round from the prize money.

Match Loser's Back, especially if he's the one whose performance lost his side the team weight, can be recognised by the number of rod rests sticking out of it. If he's blown a really big event, he staggers into the surgery looking like a fugitive from Custer's Last Stand.

Match Winner's Neck is a dislocation resulting from its failure to support its owner's recently inflated head. There is no known cure until the swelling goes down. All he can do is buy a cap three sizes bigger.

There is the story about the match winner who went home all despondent. He said to his wife, 'Since I won that match, love, all the lads are calling me Bighead.'

'Take no notice, Pet. They're only jealous. To take your mind off it, nip down to the shops and get ten pounds of potatoes.'

'Right, love. Where's the shopping bag?'

'Oh, you won't need that. Put them in your cap.'

Match Loser's Neck is also a dislocation, this time resulting from the ministrations of his stalwart comrades with a length of rope and a convenient tree.

Match Loser's Head is a severe flattening on top, caused by being bashed with everything from half a brick to a two-pound hammer, and can be recognised by the way the angler's cap keeps falling over his eyes.

* * *

Welly Toe comes from putting the wellies on the wrong feet first thing in the morning, and then refusing to switch them because it's unlucky. Either that or forgetting to take out the chunks of hard cheese you left in your wellies after the last trip so you'd know where to find them next time.

Perhaps the most painful affliction of all is *Boater's Hernia*, caused by the angler having one foot on the bank and one foot in the boat when the boat moves away. Some things can be stretched only so far.

One way of avoiding this is to leap from the boat to the bank, but if the boat moves away under the force of the leap, as it invariably does, then severe *Waterlogging* can set in. The only effective First Aid treatment for this is to find a pub with a mangle. (No use sitting in the spin-dryer: you come out too dizzy to drink your Scotch.)

I'm lucky, I suppose. Most of my boating is done with Doc Thumper, ol' buddy mate and physician extraordinary. He's very good at treating hernias and waterlogging. But I'd rather not keep putting him to all that trouble.

The shame of it

Dear Uncle Clifford,

Oh dear, the fat's really in the fire now. As you know, my mother was never in favour of my going out with an angler, but my father was very keen on the idea. It would be nice to have someone in the family he could go fishing with, he said, instead of being surrounded by indifference and hostility.

So when Sidney came round to meet my parents I was looking forward to him and my father hitting it off. And they did hit it off for half an hour or so, talking animatedly over tea about their respective triumphs on the canal.

'Funny, though,' said my father. 'I've never seen you at any of the matches or club functions.'

'No,' said Sidney. 'I've never seen you, either. Strange, that. The Waltonians have lots of social activities.'

That did it.

'The Waltonians?' bellowed Father, who as I've mentioned is a member of Slagville Piscatorials. (It hadn't crossed my mind that they were the Waltonians' deadly rivals.) 'That bunch of bloody deadbeats? Couldn't catch a cold, any of 'em. I've spit better fishermen than that lot!'

'Steady on. That's a bit strong,' said Sidney. 'What club are you in, then?'

'What club? The *only* one! The Piscatorials!'

'The Piscatorials?' Sidney yelled, a vein in his forehead throbbing ominously. 'Bloody wallies! They couldn't catch typhoid in an epidemic! Half of 'em are so doddery they can't lift a rod without risking a hernia!'

'I'll tell you something, you cheeky young bugger,' said father, 'I'm having no flaming Waltonian in this family, and that's flat!'

'And I'll tell you something, you silly old sod,' said Sidney. 'I wouldn't belong to any family that had a Piscatorial within a mile of it. And who said anything about coming into this crummy family anyway?'

At this point events took a turn for the worse. Several turns, actually.

I burst into tears.

My father squashed a chocolate eclair in Sidney's face.

My mother hit Father over the head with the best teapot. Luckily it was empty by this time, but even so the tea-leaves made quite a mess on the carpet as it shattered.

Sidney flung back his chair, stormed out of the house, and drove off without so much as a backward glance. My father attempted to grab him as he went out of the door, but Mother laid him low with a well-aimed set of ornamental fire-irons. Father, not Sidney.

I am now in a terrible state. The love of my life has swept out and left me. Father and Mother are fighting hammer-and-tongs every hour on the hour – when Father isn't down at the club, that is, telling his cronies how he sorted out that cheeky young yobbo who impugned the good name of the Piscatorials.

What on earth shall I do? Surely this kind of thing doesn't go on in other households?

Worried Blue Eyes

Dear Worried Blue Eyes,

It goes on all the time. The number of wedding receptions which end in a free-for-all because the bride and groom's families belong to rival angling clubs is incalculable, and added to every weekend.

Time is a great healer, if you'll pardon the platitude. It is possible that your father and Sidney will see the error of their ways, agree to differ, let sleeping dogs lie, bury the hatchet and smoke the pipe of peace. So far in angling's history there's no record of such a reconciliation, but there's always a first time for everything.

Other possible solutions are that your father can be persuaded to join the Waltonians. Or that Sidney will transfer his allegiance to the Piscatorials. Or that the two clubs will amalgamate, thus removing the clash of loyalties. Or that pigs might fly.

You and Sidney could elope, perhaps, and live far enough away to preclude any accidental meeting between him and your father. Tristan da Cunha offers excellent sea fishing, and property prices are reasonable on account of the occasional volcanic eruption.

Or perhaps you should find another feller. And check this time. Silly moo.

A shock to the system

Fishing is supposed to be relaxing, supposed to be an aid to peace of mind and long life. But I'm beginning to wonder.

There was this doddery old boy I met on the bank. Shaking in every limb, he was, wrinkled like a crab-apple and the hair of his head and beard snow white. But there he was, fishing peacefully away.

'To what do you attribute your great age?' I asked.

'Fishing,' he said.

'Marvellous,' I said.

'Fishing,' he said. 'And booze. And wimmin.'

'Even better,' I said. 'And how old are you?'

'Thirty-three.'

* * *

No, I just made that up. But I have come across several cases in which fishing has brought a hell of a shock to the participants. And probably knocked several years off their lives.

It knocked quite a few years off the natural span of an angler in Melbourne, Australia. (All right. I know *you* know where Melbourne is, but not everybody's that well up on the Antipodes.)

All his life he had dreamed of a giant catch. He got one: a 58lb cod. As he landed it he dropped down dead.

His loving wife gave a funeral tea which befitted the passing of such a dedicated angler. It was a supper, actually: a fish supper. Cod fritters on a bed of clams with the departed's name written in instant mashed potato over the lot. Doubtless just as he would have wished.

* * *

Katie Crowe, of Dallas, Texas, had four shocks in a row when she went fishing on a charter boat out of Miami, Florida, with her husband, Charlie. (Charlie's got nothing to do with the story. Don't know why I mentioned him really.)

Only minutes after Katie had said to the mate that she'd never caught a sailfish, the mate yelled, 'You've caught a sailfish!'

That was Shock No. 1.

Shock No. 2 came when she reeled in the fish after a 20-minute fight. It was dead. Drowned, said the crew, on account of the spirited struggle it put up.

It hadn't seemed like much of a struggle to Katie. More like a dead weight, spinning in the wake with the speed of the boat.

Anyway, back on shore Katie agreed to have it mounted at a cost of £215 (in dollars). But in stepped some suspicious person who took the fish round to a scientist.

Then came Shock No. 3. The scientist pronounced the fish not only dead, but having been that way and kept on ice for 12 hours before being returned to the water.

Shock No. 4 came when some spoilsports from another boat reported seeing the mate fix the sailfish to the line and throw it in the water.

The boat's skipper, while denying such scurrilous charges, did admit that there was nothing which filled him with greater joy than seeing satisfied customers on their way to the trophy-mounting shop.

It's the kind of thing that could only happen in the States. But is it? It does not behove us upright Britons to cast nasturtiums and point the finger of scorn. The number of dead fish landed in some of our matches cannot always be attributed to natural causes or reasonable wear and tear. It comes as a shock to the stewards to discover this. And comes as a greater shock to the naughty angler who has landed them when he is taken behind the weighing-in shed by members of the opposition for a quiet ticking-off and mayhap a few knuckle butties.

* * *

The next bit is not as dramatic as the foregoing examples, but it was enough to cope with at the time.

I was fishing a lake near Leighton Buzzard when a lady person came running up in a state of great distress.

'Come and help me, please,' she said. 'My husband's had a heart attack and he's liable to fall down the bank.'

61

Up rose the gallant Parker, wellies pounding, and raced to where this bloke was doing a very good imitation of a Dear Departed. He was sprawled halfway down a steep bank, at the bottom of which was a sizeable pike doing the conga in a landing net.

I almost became a fully paid-up corpse myself, getting him up the bank and spread out on the grass.

'Don't panic,' I said to the distraught lady person. 'Have no fear. Parker's here. I will dash and get help.'

That bit was easier said than done. The lake was in the middle of some really rough pastureland, and there was a quarter of a mile of winding sheep track between me and my faithful motor-car. Pant pant. Get to the road. Zoom off in faithful motor-car to find phone-box. None about. Sheep don't have much call for phone-boxes.

Finally arrive at village. Into cop-shop containing two large police persons. Police persons ring for ambulance, then follow me in *der-der* car back to sheep track. Ambulance arrives with stretcher on trolley. Police and ambulance persons push trolley down track. All arrive at lakeside red-faced and puffed out.

To find bloke sitting calmly on bank gazing admiringly at pike, now in keep net.

'Sorry to have bothered you,' he said. 'It was nothing really. I'm perfectly all right now.'

Ambulance persons start pushing trolley back up sheep track to road. Larger of police persons, sweating profusely, brings out notebook.

'What did you say your name was?' he asks, fixing me with official stony-type stare. 'Parker? I'll remember that.'

When the police persons had gone, the lady person made her apologies.

'Awfully sorry,' she said. 'I keep telling him but he takes no notice. He always gets so excited when he catches a pike. I'm sure it can't be doing him any good.'

Parker muttering, through pain of straining lungs and incipient hernia, 'Think nothing of it. Glad to have been of service.' But fixing bloke with unofficial stony-type stare and thinking, 'Next time, you old twit, you can drop down dead.'

* * *

When you've got to go, you've got to go – and flaking out with the excitement of playing a big fish is a better way to go than most – but I'd rather stay.

I mentioned this to Tactful Tetters.

'I shouldn't worry,' he said. 'Since when did you ever catch anything to get excited about?'

Cheek. But should it come to pass that I am struck down battling with the Monster of Idiots' Reach, I shall certainly not entrust the disposal of my mortal remains to Tetters.

Recently he carried out the last wishes of an old sea-fishing pal: to cast his ashes into the sea off Filey Brigg in Yorkshire. He and a few mates of the old lad went to the edge of the Brigg, but met with what felt like a gale blowing in from the sea. They walked along for a bit until they found a spot which seemed more sheltered than the others.

From there, Tetters cast in the old lad's ashes, consigning them to the deep. But just then the wind veered and found the sheltered spot. The ashes went flying back over the Brigg, most of them finishing up in the butties of a family having a picnic.

Perhaps it was not quite as Tetters' old mate would have wished, but it wasn't far from it. He cast from the top of Filey Brigg, certainly. The only difference was that his last resting place was not the storm-tossed waters of the North Sea, but a couple of cheese-and-pickle butties.

That's who it was, if anyone picnicking on Filey Brigg noticed that the butties were a bit gritty. No, don't go 'Bleargh!' He was a nice old lad ...

All manglers great and small

Remember that marvellous television series *Life on Earth*, in which David Attenborough went through all the life forms from the primaeval sludge to brain surgeons?

Great stuff. What I found particularly interesting was how the marsupials, the really primitive mammals with pouches, have developed independently in remote places into counterparts of higher mammals in other parts of the world. There are marsupial equivalents of mice, rats, cats, bears, moles, anteaters, squirrels, deer – even a marsupial wolf which seems to be no longer with us on account of conservation-minded Aussies using it for target practice.

What these strange animals demonstrate is that if a certain physical pattern is suited to a certain lifestyle, Nature makes sure that this pattern develops.

It is a little known fact – a totally unknown fact, in fact – that there is an order of British marsupial living in the Lost Islands of Lankiland, between Blackpool and Wigan, which has developed completely independently of other British wildlife. The Lost Islands have been isolated for thousands of years on account of being surrounded first of all by water, and then by a broad belt of agricultural land in which there is not a pub for miles.

The staple diet of these marsupials is fish, and they have therefore developed into different forms of primitive angler, with remarkable parallels to the anglers of the outside world.

These bizarre creatures are to be scientifically classified as Manglers, short for Marsupial Anglers.

Most common is the *Common Mangler*, which possibly comes as no surprise. The male is medium-sized, nondescript to tatty in appearance, with a pair of short stubby legs for jamming in wellies.

Its prey is anything daft enough to fall for its clumsy fishing methods, and its pouch is stuffed with an assortment of maggies, lobs, bread, cheese and bits of sausage. It also carries a few spinners, which accounts for the pained look which occasionally crosses its face and its habit of suddenly leaping six feet in the air.

The real surprise is that this species *is* so common. The appearance of the male is enough to send females screaming off into the blue, and his mating call of 'Give-us-a-kiss-love-I've-put-me-teeth-in' can hardly be called irresistible.

There are several more specialised varieties of Mangler, each adapted to a particular life pattern.

STAR-NOSED MANGLER
↓

SHOW-OFF OR KOKKYSOD MANGLER
↓

The *Star-nosed Mangler* can be recognised by its lurching gait and its bulbous, fluorescent nose which can sniff out a barman's apron at a thousand yards. It spends only a little of its time fishing. As soon as the pubs open, its inbuilt biological clock goes 'Drrringgg! Drrringgg!' and the antennae on top of its head swivel to get a fix on the nearest boozer.

This creature has a permanently dry tongue and parched throat, but Nature has compensated by giving it a capacious gullet which can sink a pint every ten seconds. Because it has to endure long periods of drought – sometimes as much as five hours – its pouch is capacious enough to take one, sometimes two, crates of ale.

The *Ace Match Mangler* has a furtive manner and eyes which swivel suspiciously all around. Its crêpe-soled feet enable it to creep up silently behind other manglers and its big floppy ears help it to overhear discussions on likely baits and swims.

Its own baits it keeps very secret, and buries them in the depths of its double-locked pouch. When asked the secrets of its success, it taps its nose with a forefinger and says with a mysterious smile, 'That'd be telling.' When it's in a good mood, that is. In a bad mood it replies, 'What the hell's that got to do with you? Bugger off.'

The *Match Fiddler Mangler* has a pouch lined with plastic bags to hold dead fish, spiral leads and bars of soap. Its right forefinger is about 24 inches long, to enable it to hold down undetected the pan of the scales at the weigh-in.

When challenged it adopts a submissive posture and emits a plaintive cry of 'Who? Me?' When it sees that it can bluff no longer it takes flight, aided in a quick getaway by the spikes on the soles of its feet.

The principal enemy of the Fiddler Mangler is the *Steward Mangler*. This is a cold, cruel, pitiless creature which stalks the bank with a stiff-legged gait and one arm stuck up in the air. Other recognition points are its little moustache, drooping forelock and raucous cries of '*Sieg Heil!*'

When it sees a likely victim, it first paralyses it with cries of 'Off the bank! This minute! Off! Off!' and then belabours it with a sockful of damp sand produced from its pouch. Occasionally, especially on a quiet day, its selectivity is impaired and it may belabour perfectly innocent Common Manglers.

Less aggressive, but still not to be trifled with, is the *Bailiff Mangler*. This creature has telescopic eyesight, a quiet tread, and a coat which blends into almost any background. It is expert in the arts of lurking, stalking and pouncing, and has two methods of dealing with its prey. Initially it makes understanding noises: if these do not produce the desired result, it puts the welly in.

The Bailiff Mangler's pouch contains a set of rules for the water, indicating that every known method of taking fish is prohibited, and several books of tickets for all the dud stretches. The creature has a sadistic habit of making sure the victim buys a ticket before announcing that the stretch has not yielded a fish since records began.

The *No-ticket Hedge-hopping Mangler* fears no other creature but the Bailiff. Distinguishing features of this marsupial are the sharp eyes and pricked-up ears, with which it detects the Bailiff's approach, and the kangaroo-like legs with which it makes its escape. When cornered, it will produce from its pouch a sheaf of out-of-date tickets which it has previously collected from the bank, and utter plaintive cries of, 'I-know-I-had-it-here-this-morning'.

The *Show-off* or *Kokkysod Mangler* is easily recognised by its gaudy coat and size $10\frac{7}{8}$ bobbly hat festooned with badges. Its cry is loud and consists mainly of, 'That's-nothing-you-should-have-seen-what-I-got-last-week'. Its pouch is full of photographs of enormous fish, most of them caught by somebody else.

Perhaps the strangest creature of all is the *Scribbling Mangler*, which exists by trading odd scraps of information for food. Its pouch is full of yellowed press cuttings and stubs of pencil.

It has one large ear and one small one. The large one is used for picking up ideas and cries of 'What's yours?' The small one, the deaf one, is tuned to cries of, 'Hey – have you heard the joke about . . .' or – even worse – 'Come on, Parker. Your round.'

Sidney gets coarse

Dear Uncle Clifford,

I'm sure Father would never even consider joining the Sludge-thorpe Waltonians; he's far too set in his ways. And I would never even consider getting another 'feller' as you so quaintly put it. But getting Sidney to join the Slagville Piscatorials sounds an excellent idea. I think, however, that perhaps the time is not ripe to suggest it.

I saw Sidney after work the next day and we both agreed that the rift between him and my father should not affect our relationship. He said he didn't mean it about mine being a crummy family – only my dad was crummy. So that's all right; neither Mother nor I would disagree with that.

Sidney and I are just the victims of circumstance; star-crossed lovers, like Romeo and Juliet. I told Sidney about the feud between the Montagues and Capulets, thinking he would see the resemblance to our situation, but all he wanted to know was who they fished for. I don't think Shakespeare mentioned it in the play.

The bliss of our reunion was short-lived, however, because of the onset of the new coarse season. Sidney kept muttering about the 'Glorious 16th', and at first I thought he'd taken up shooting or something. Then he would go round singing a little song he'd made up, and doing Jimmy Durante imitations:

> *Tinc . . .*
> *A-tinca-doo . . .*
> *A-tinca dee a-tinca doo . . .*

Sidney doesn't look much like Jimmy Durante, except around the nose, but I had to admit he was quite good. He explained that *Tinca tinca* is the Latin name for tench, traditionally the first fish of the coarse season. He went into raptures about its splendid fighting qualities, given to it by its broad tail; its beautiful colouring and distinctive eyes. He said a tench's eyes were like mine, which I took as a great compliment and which led to my surrendering to his charms.

Later, as we lay contentedly in each other's arms, he spoiled everything.

'Darling,' I whispered, frankly fishing for further compliments, 'tell me more about the tench's eyes. What are they like?'

Sidney thought for a while before he spoke.

'A tench's eyes? Now let me see ... They're sort of ... er ... bloodshot.'

Well, that did it, I can tell you. Took all the romance out of the evening. I belaboured him with a rolled-up copy of *Angling Times* (the bumper pre-season issue, which was quite heavy) and swept off home in floods of tears.

I have not seen him since to speak to, on account of the season's opening. Work is not the place to approach him and demand an apology, and on top of that he has been off for several days with a severe attack of hay fever. Presumably, this time, having run out of grandmas for good and all.

Please, Uncle Clifford, tell me about the tench's eyes. What colour are they? Are they really bloodshot? I must admit that mine have been lately, because of all the crying I have done, and my nose is a bit red at the end. But I'm sure they're not bloodshot normally.

Put me out of my misery. Tell me they're not really bloodshot. Or tell me the awful truth, so that I can do something about it or at least accept it as a cruel trick of Nature.

Worried Blue Eyes

Dear Worried Blue Eyes,

The tench has the most marvellous eyes of any freshwater fish. A sort of reddish-gold colour, they are, and very beautiful. They give the impression of a fish of great wisdom and knowledge, holding secrets too deep for mere *homo sapiens* to fathom.

That's what Sidney really meant. That your eyes have the rich, warm glow of African gold. That they are full of mystery; deep with wisdom, as old as time, and possessing a rare and irresistible enchantment.

That's what he meant. Get him to tell you when his early-season fever has abated a little. The inarticulate little pillock.

Getting the taste for it

Kevin Maddocks and his mate John Baker said just about everything there is to say about groundbaits for carp in their book *Carp Fever*. However, in the interests of science and to enlarge the scope of the debate, I'd like to throw in my own two penn'orth about Groundbaits for All Seasons.

Kevin and John say that the best way to test a groundbait for flavour is to chew a small piece. When you're satisfied, they say, spit it out.

Good advice, that. You never know where it's been. But sometimes it tastes so good that it seems a shame to waste it.

As well as tasting the stuff myself, I get reactions from other discerning parties, such as the cat. Daft Cat has many peculiarities, but one of the strangest is her love for groundbait.

Every week there are one or two half-full tins of different flavoured catfoods in the fridge, abandoned because she's gone off those particular flavours and refused to touch them. But as soon as they're mashed up with the bread and bran, she's there, yarling for a bit. The speed with which she shifts it is usually a good indication of its fish-appeal. I try some on the birds in the garden, too. If a plateful's gone within fifteen minutes, it's OK.

One of my finest efforts included some time-expired black puddings. I stuck the mixture outside in a bucket to cool. When I went to collect it, there was next-door's daft dog, raising its head from the empty bucket with a vulgar but grateful 'Urrrpp!'

Obviously a successful mix. Pity there wasn't enough left for conclusive proof.

Another test of a good formula is what happens to it on the bank. Apart from wandering dogs, ducks and assorted tweety-birds diving in for a sample, I've had water voles, squirrels and even rats chomping away a couple of feet from my right welly.

I don't let them go too far, mind you. Once they've proved that the stuff tastes good, I get on with the landing-net-handle-and-ferocious-oaths routine.

One of the finest additives is Doctor Dumdum's Electric Wonder Oil, of which by now you're probably sick of hearing but which really does work. As you're also sick of hearing, Mad Mac bought supplies in bulk from a little Indian with a turban in a pub.

Trouble is that stocks are now running low and we have to be very sparing with it. We've searched every pub for miles for a little Indian with a turban, but the only one we found was selling telescopic umbrellas and silk neckties. Nowt wrong with the umbrellas, and the ties were very tasteful, but not a lot of use for our purpose.

*   *   *

The run-up to Christmas is a good time for free additives to the groundbait. All the stuff left over from office parties and works outings. Sausages on sticks, vol-au-vents, crackers, cheese and what have you. No shame in sticking it in a doggy bag and taking it home.

I've even tried in pubs, at the end of a lunchtime session, asking if I could relieve them of the curling butties in the glass case. No luck there, though. The usual reply from a publican advertising fresh-cut sandwiches is: 'Get lost. Them's for tonight.'

At any function it's always best to make sure stuff *is* left over before you appropriate it. Many an angler's wedding has been ruined because his mates were discovered nicking great chunks of cake at the reception. (Currants, raisins, spices, marzipan and icing-sugar, apart from anything else. What fish could resist that lot?)

Opposition to the purloining seems to come mainly from the bride's mother. The bride's father is either very understanding, especially if he's an angler himself, or too far gone to care.

Whichever way you look at it, though, nicking wedding-cake is highly reprehensible and unworthy of the angling fraternity. It's usually the first-timers who are caught, because they sit there wrapping it in paper napkins and shoving it into their pockets. The more experienced nickers stick it swiftly behind a curtain and collect it later. So I'm told.

Maddocks and Baker recommend Paxo stuffings among the list of savoury additives for carp groundbait. That's OK, but as Christmas draws nearer it's best to check with the wife first. If she's hunting frantically around on Christmas morning, with the bread rubbed and the onions boiled, and not a packet of Paxo in sight, you may not be the most popular man in the world.

Glad I mentioned the bread. A couple of Christmases ago, I found two loaves going stale on top of the bread bin. Magic. Big bucket of groundbait in no time. But my reception when I got home that night was a bit on the frosty side. The loaves had been left to go stale to make the stuffing.

Best to check anyway before you use anything from the kitchen. I did a roundup of the goodies once. Sweetcorn, bread, sausages, tin of luncheon meat, couple of black puddings and some other odds and ends.

When I got home I gave the traditional greeting: 'Where's me tea?'

'I wouldn't swear to it,' said Dearly Beloved. 'But I think you've spent all day chucking it in the canal.'

Ho ho. *Very* droll . . .

A clean sheet

I'm well pleased when along comes June 16th and the start of the coarse fishing season. But possibly not half as pleased as Dearly Beloved, who reckons that three months is a long time to spend under her feet, looking as if I'd just lost a quid at a funeral.

Don't know what Dearly Beloved's complaining about anyway. Missis Mad Mac has been giving him money and sending him off to the pub all through the close season, just to get him out of the way. Suggestions that my perambulations also might be encouraged by some small donation were treated with scorn and derision, the gist of the reply being that I didn't need any encouragement to go to the boozer.

In spite of such shabby – not to say harsh – treatment, a touch of remorse did set in as I pondered on what Dearly Beloved puts up with during the season. I resolved therefore to be A Better Man.

I resolved also to lighten the load of all angling wives by making you lot Better Men. (Don't see why I should be the only one to suffer.) And to that end have formulated a set of New Season Resolutions.

So raise your right hands and repeat after me:

I solemnly swear . . .

1. Before the start of the season I shall cut the grass, hack a bit off the hedge and tickle round the veg patch.

2. I shall not nick from the kitchen, without prior agreement, any tins of luncheon meat, sweetcorn, frankfurters or pussycat food.

3. I shall not place in the fridge any noxious concoctions of a high pong content, nor any tins of over-excitable maggies, without first double-wrapping and labelling them conspicuously. (Although they *are* quite tasty, maggies are no real substitute for long grain rice, even in curries.)

4. I shall slide out of bed on dawn trips as unobtrusively as possible, and will have laid out my clobber downstairs. (This

avoids getting dressed in the dark, getting both feet down one trouser leg, falling flat on one's face and disturbing the quiet of the morning with oaths and imprecations.)

5. Having arrived downstairs, I shall close the door behind me to confine the sound of the early morning coughing fit. I shall also take special care not to step on Daft Cat.

6. I shall creep out through the back door and close it silently behind me. (The back door, as well as being further from the bedroom, is also free from milk bottles, a hazard one tends to forget in the excitement of setting out.)

7. Once outside, I shall refrain from singing, whistling or tap dancing until well clear of human habitation.

8. On the bank I shall conduct myself with decorum and show every consideration to fellow anglers. Especially big ones with tattooed knuckles. Thus ensuring a return home with all the teeth I set out with.

9. At the end of the day I shall resist the temptation to allow intemperate acquaintances to lead me astray. (In my case, Mad Mac and Big McGinty. Just substitute the names of your own Bad Influences.)

10. Should I fail to resist the temptation I shall approach the old homestead with dignity and in silence, refraining from bursting into song however full of cheer I may be.

11. On the way home I shall buy a small gift for my Ever Loving as a token of my appreciation of her tolerance and forbearance. Money shall be no object, unless it gets to more than 50p.

12. I shall have bidden an Angler's Farewell to Bad Influences (Mad Mac and Big McGinty again) some distance from home. This will prevent their bursting into the house with large cans and the odd bottle of hard stuff, expecting Dearly Beloved to produce a couple of trays of instant butties.

13. I shall enter the house by the back door (the milk bottles are bound to be out again at the front), having first dumped my tackle, outer clobber and wellies in the shed.

14. Should Dearly Beloved have retired to bed, and the place be in darkness, I shall once again take care not to step on the family pet (in my case Daft Cat). And shall ascend the stairs

with as much caution as is compatible with my state of mind and the lack of illumination.

15. Above all, I shall not get into bed upside down. (Such a small miscalculation, easily made in a moment of temporary disorientation, causes no end of trouble and can bring observance of all the previous resolutions to naught.)

* * *

There you are, lads. Keep that lot up and your wives won't know you.

Keep that lot up and nobody will know you.

Two sides to everything

There are two sides to everything, I always say. Unless it's a triangle, in which case it's the exception which proves the rule. It depends on which way you look at it, I always say.

I am always saying wise things such as these, and sometimes I'm so clever I make myself sick.

What's brought this on is that I've been out on a boat on the Thames, looking at anglers from the other side.

Doc Thumper's boat it was (and still is, in spite of everything). A sleek 22-footer with a cabin and a Calor gas stove, an engine at the back and a proper little steering wheel on the bridge.

Doc Thumper, ol' buddy mate and physician extraordinary, is well hooked on things nautical.

'Ahoy there,' he said on the electric telephone. 'Avast and belay! We up anchor on the morning tide.'

. . . Down at the boatyard, Doc was looking very seamanlike, with bell-bottomed trousers and a seafaring hat on his head. (The bell-bottomed trousers did look a bit daft on his head, but he'll soon get the hang of it.) I made my own contribution with a Popeye badge and a rolling gait.

'Welcome aboard,' said Doc, producing a bottle of Bell's. 'This is a happy ship.'

'That,' I said as I spliced a treble mainbrace, 'I can well believe.'

Doc's Number One Son had already run the colours up the mast – a West Bromwich Albion ensign, which doubtless one day will find its way into the Admiralty catalogue of recognition flags – and the boat was ready for a following wind and a favourable tide.

'Cast off fore, aft and ift,' commanded Doc, getting with the ancient Goon Show jokes. 'My compliments to Mr Parker and how does he suggest we get under way?'

'Reef your t'gallants, luff your stuns'ls and shake out the mains'l,' I said, having just read a Hornblower book.

'Tricky,' said Doc. 'We haven't got any sails. We'll have to use the engine.'

'Bejabers,' I said, lapsing into an old Irish joke. 'We'll never get that thing to the top of the mast.'

We set a course west by nor' nor' west, which was convenient because that's the way the river was pointing.

'The wind's backing to the nor'ard,' shouted Doc over the crash of the waves.

'I'm sorry about that,' I said. 'It's this Chinese food.'

'Can you see ahead?' asked Doc.

'Yes,' I said. 'A dirty great bald one.'

Which was the end of the Goon Show routines. And not before time.

We were doing very well, in spite of having to drive on the right, which was made more difficult by my having to steer one-handed. (How else could I drink the Scotch?) We stopped doing well when we met a smaller version of the *QE2* coming the other way.

'Hard a-starboard!' shouted Doc.

'Which way's that?'

'Right, you barmy bugger!'

(Such unprofessional language. Whatever happened to his bedside manner?)

Hard a-starboard I went. A bit too close to the bank for comfort, though we missed it thanks to my superb seamanship. And then it happened.

From the undergrowth along the bank erupted weird and frightening apparitions. Almost human in form, but gap-toothed, tattooed, hairy and wearing outlandish tribal dress.

They leapt frenziedly up and down, screaming wild oaths and imprecations and throwing all sorts of deadly missiles at our fragile craft.

'Hard a-port!' shouted Doc. 'Left, to you!'

'Gad,' I said, torn between punitive action and desertion, 'the natives are restless tonight.'

'I don't like the cut of their jib,' said Doc. 'Can you identify them?'

From the few words of *patois* I could distinguish, and from

79

the notice-board on the bank, I was fairly certain.

'London Anglers Association. A very warlike tribe when provoked.'

* * *

Funny, isn't it? From the bridge, all I could see was a bunch of hairy yobboes making a fuss about nothing, and certainly with no appreciation of the hazards of navigation or the finer arts of seamanship.

But a couple of days later Doc and I were sitting on the bank, gently fishing and generally minding our own business. All of a sudden, along came a boat piloted by some drunken capitalist swine. It was swerving about much too close to the bank, sending the keep nets swinging around, scaring off the fish and just missing our lines.

Doc and I were on our feet, leaping from the undergrowth, jumping frenziedly up and down, screaming wild oaths and imprecations and throwing all sorts of ineffectual missiles at the heavily armoured craft.

There are two sides to everything, I always say. And a lot seems to depend which one you're on at the time . . .

* * *

From a mate called Fred I have learned about the ultimate deterrent for anti-social weekend sailors.

Fred was float legering when a power boat came along, aimed straight at the float and cut the line. Fred grabbed his tin of maggots, ran upstream to the next bridge, waited till the power boat passed underneath and then let it have the lot.

The great thing, apparently, is that not only does the skipper person get covered in maggies, and have to spend ages getting them out of his hair, underpants, socks and dolly bird. And then have to chase the others for hours all over the deck. Not only that – but hundreds of them will have escaped meantime into the bilges . . . and for a good few weeks the boat will be a floating bluebottle farm.

I like it, I like it. It's hard being saintly *all* the time. It occurs to me that sometimes I'm a very evil person. Now and again I worry about it.

Every man has his price

Dear Uncle Clifford,

I cannot thank you too much. When Sidney's fishing fever had abated enough for us to be speaking again, I showed him your reply about the tench's eyes and he said it was exactly what he meant.

It was all right for that old bum, he said (meaning you, I'm afraid), thinking up flowery phrases in the monastic calm of his book-lined study, but he had to answer on the spur of the moment. He meant to say, 'suffused with a golden glow', but it came out as 'bloodshot'. And he says he's not inarticulate; his father and mother got married eventually.

A little later I mentioned your earlier suggestion that he should join Slagville Piscatorials as a step towards a reconciliation between him and Father.

No way, he said. Never in a million years. He wouldn't be seen dead with that lot. No power on earth could force him. He was so adamant that I thought my hopes had been dashed for ever. Sidney is a man of iron once his mind is made up.

Imagine my surprise when, a week later, he told me he had joined the Piscatorials.

I asked him what had brought about this sudden change of heart. Had he done it just to please me? Was it because of our deep and undying love, strong enough to break down all barriers, overcome all obstacles, climb every mountain, swim every sea? Could he no longer resist the pleading, passionate look in my eyes as I begged him to make the ultimate sacrifice for my sake?

You could say that, said Sidney. But it was more the fact that he'd discovered that the Piscatorials' bar prices were a lot cheaper than the Waltonians', and with a wider selection of ales. Also the fact that they'd taken a lease on the flash behind our plastics factory: a lot easier to get to from work, holding some nice pike and just stocked with a good head of fair-sized bream.

And he hadn't left the Sludgethorpe Waltonians. He was very proud of the club and its fine sporting traditions, most of his mates were members, and besides which he'd just coughed up for a year's subs. If he couldn't stand the Piscatorials, as he suspected might be the case, he wouldn't have put all his eggs in one basket, burned all his bridges, or cut off his nose to spite his face.

His entry into the Piscatorials was not all plain sailing. Apparently my father had made strong representations to the membership committee against Sidney's acceptance, and even threatened to resign if my beloved was allowed to join.

Father's objections were overruled on the grounds that the club was in a membership drive to help pay for the lease on the flash, and that they'd been hoping for years that he would resign because of the fuss he made over the results at every match weigh-in.

Father didn't carry out his threat, of course, because it would have ruined his social life, but he still came home in a very bad mood, refused to eat his tea, and kicked the cat unmercifully.

My mother is quite fond of Sidney now, even though she objected to my going out with an angler in the first place. Any lad, she says, who gets up Father's nose like that can't be all bad.

And nobody can say that Sidney hasn't tried. What moral torment he must have suffered in joining the Piscatorials, even though their bar prices are cheaper, nobody will ever know.

So that really only leaves my father. What can I do to get him to see reason, to help restore an atmosphere of peace and harmony, to have him accept Sidney as a potential son-in-law?

Worried Blue Eyes

Dear Worried Blue Eyes,

Try to get your father in a good mood and to keep him that

way. A few feminine wiles are all you need. Make sure there's always a cup of tea ready for him when he comes home, that his pipe and slippers are by the fireplace, that you don't leave your undies festooning the bathroom, and don't hog the telephone.

If that doesn't work, you might have to consider something more drastic, such as poisoning the old bugger.

The best part of the day

The big snag for me about summer fishing is the time you have to get up. It hurts. And sometimes it hurts Dearly Beloved more than it hurts me.

I can never knock off the alarm clock at the first attempt. I generally juggle it all over the bedroom and finish up kicking it against the wall.

'For goodness' sake, Clifford John! Can't you do *anything* quietly?' comes the wail from the trainee corpse under the bedclothes.

'Sorry, Petal,' I say, booting the clock out onto the landing. 'I can't help it if I'm not mechanically-minded.'

At one time we had one of those tea-making machines which wakes you up and has a pot of tea ready. I stopped using that after I tripped over it one morning. The room was filled with flashing lights and ringing bells. A gusher of boiling water shot from the thing and did severe damage to my person in an area in which I would rather not have severe damage done.

When Number One Son was younger it was easy. He'd get up, collect the bait and tackle, and bring a mug of tea to his groaning old papa. But as soon as he discovered girls, the cold light of dawn lost its appeal.

My old dad was the best. He was in the wholesale green-grocery business and in the strawberry season thought nothing of getting up at three in the morning. I didn't think much of it either.

'Wakey-wakey!' he'd bellow cheerfully. 'Best time of day, this is!'

He could have fooled me.

The next hazard after the alarm clock is Daft Cat. If I don't feed her straightaway she's under my feet, tripping me up when I'm trying to brew a pot of tea, doing more severe damage to my person. If I put the boot in, as is occasionally my wont, she's upstairs complaining to Dearly Beloved and I cop it again.

After a pint of tea and a good cough, I'm generally approaching consciousness. As an aid to quicker recovery I tried some herbal tea I found in a health food shop. *Morning Thunder*, this tea's called, and it certainly lives up to its name. I stopped using it after complaints from the Noise Abatement Society.

Full consciousness is essential if you are to arrive at the waterside with everything you intended. Number One Son and I once walked four miles to the canal with baskets and nets, and realised it would have been much more worth while if one of us had remembered the rods.

Getting out of the house without waking up the neighbourhood is difficult. However hard I try, Sod's Law always sets in. The Law decrees that if I close the front door still draped in tackle and gear, it locks itself on the end of the holdall or the rim of the keep net.

This is inevitably the time I've forgotten the key, so I've got to bang on the door and wake up Dearly Beloved. Long-suffering girl though she is, she is not exactly thrilled at having to stagger downstairs in her nightie. Just as she thought the old duffer had finally got himself out of the house.

If ever I divest myself of the tackle on the doorstep and turn round to close the door quietly, there's a sudden gust of wind and the damn thing slams shut, rattling every window in the house and a few next door. Now and again, before I can do a thing to the door, I'm left sprawling on the deck because Daft Cat has run out between my wellies to answer a passionate call from one of her fleabitten boyfriends.

But now and again I manage it. Door shut quietly. Tackle intact and untrapped. Smirking, I turn round to head off into the Wild Blue Yonder. And go swingtip over pinkies in a crash of empty milk bottles.

For all that, I usually manage to get out, equipped with most if not all of the essentials, and eventually get to the water. Not like somebody who shall be nameless. Tactful Tetters.

I'd arranged to meet him at the water, but the bank was Tettersless. Not a sign of him all through the morning. I got home in the afternoon, just as the electric telephone was ringing. Tetters.

'Sorry, our Clifford,' he said. 'I had rather a hard day last night and I've just come round. My clock's stopped as well and –'

'You're a bit late,' I said. 'I've been and come back. It's half past four.'

'Most obliged,' he said. 'But could we start at the beginning. It's not so much the time I'm worried about. What *day* is it?'

Another fine mess

'That's another fine mess you got me into,' said Doc Thumper, waving his plaster cast dangerously near the aristocratic Parker hooter.

'Never touched you,' I said. 'How did you come to get your arm in plaster anyway?'

'Pigeon droppings.'

'And the same to you.'

'No,' said Doc. 'I mean you going on about putting pigeon droppings in the groundbait. I thought I'd try it. That's how I broke my arm.'

'I've never known pigeon droppings that heavy.'

'They weren't. But they were high up. On a ledge over the garage door. I fell off the ladder.'

* * *

Doc's arm was a trial to him for a few weeks. It's not easy being a one-armed GP. Patients tended to fall about when they went into the consulting room to find the medic in a worse state than they were.

It affected his fishing, too. It made baiting-up and casting very difficult. And using the landing net impossible. So for a while I was Doc's right-hand man.

Opening cans one-handed was impossible. If it hadn't been for his trusty old buddy, Doc could have suffered severe dehydration, which in extreme cases can be fatal.

Piloting his boat was tricky too. With one hand you don't get the control you need, and the craft tended to veer a lot from side to side. This resulted in the boat getting closer to the bank than was Doc's wont and causing more wash than usual, earning the occasional imprecation and half brick from anglers whose swim had been ruined.

I had to be on hand to take the vessel through the locks, leaping from the bows as to the manner born, remembering to allow enough rope to stretch to the bank. It's details like that which are the mark of the real sailor.

An addition to Doc's fishing gear, which no broken-armed angler should be without, was a plastic knitting needle. This was for scratching inside the plaster, reaching the parts that normal scratching couldn't reach.

One good thing about Doc's one-handedness was that he could no longer cook. I'm not saying he's a bad cook, but his boat's got the only rubbish-bin with ulcers. Congo pygmies make special trips to dip their arrows in his soup. It was a relief not to have to tackle greasy bacon and rubbery eggs, and to tell such lies as 'Great, this, Doc. Absolutely fantastic. Don't know how you – Groo . . .'

I was in charge of provisioning the boat. When I turned up with two bottles of Scotch and a packet of crisps, Doc went berserk.

'Can't I leave anything to you?' he demanded. 'What are we going to do with all those crisps?'

Another thing about the plaster cast was that it made it safe for us to go into angling pubs. Relations on the Upper Thames between anglers and boaters are a bit strained, and it is dangerous for anyone looking like a boater to go into a fishing pub.

Anglers are a chivalrous lot, however, and none of them would take advantage of a man with his arm in plaster. Not many of them, anyway.

I was Doc's crew for his visit to the 153 Club. This is a club consisting of people who have crossed latitude – or is it longitude? – 153 in the Sahara Desert. They were meeting at a pub near the river and Doc decided to arrive in style by boat.

The trouble with the 153 Club is that it always brings on Doc's story of the fish in the middle of the desert. When he was out there on an expedition, right in the middle of the arid wastes, as they say, he came across an oasis which was full of fish. And the odd crocodile.

They get there, apparently, through underground water courses. When the oasis disappears in a particularly dry spell, the fish and the crocodiles just go back underground. It's absolutely true, but Doc shouldn't try telling the story in a pub.

'Fish in the middle of the desert?' somebody always says. Generally an intellectual citizen weighing seventeen stone.

'Course you'd expect them, wouldn't you? Here today and gone tomorrow, eh? And crocodiles? How did you get your arm in plaster? Bumped into the Creature from the Black Lagoon, did you? If I were you, me old son, I'd take more water with it . . .'

That's one fine mess Doc gets *himself* into.

Sidney's Dark Secret

Dear Uncle Clifford,

Once again, you were so right!

I made no reference at home to Sidney, but just did what you said about having a cup of tea and pipe (packet of Woodbines, actually) and slippers ready for Father. I cleared my undies from the bathroom and stopped hogging the telephone.

Father was suspicious for a while but eventually took the treatment for granted and became much kinder to the cat. It was certainly less drastic than the other treatment you suggested, i.e. poisoning him, which was the course of action my mother favoured.

Anyway, guess what? Father and Sidney have made it up! And it's all because of Sidney's bravery and generosity.

Last week there was some jostling along the canal towpath, seemingly in the rush to get back to the Piscatorials' clubhouse and be first at the bar. Father fell in the canal and could have drowned had not Sidney rescued him by jamming a landing net over his head as he surfaced, and pulling him to safety.

At the clubhouse Sidney insisted that my father left his clothes in the boiler room to dry, lent him his knee-length anorak for decency's sake, and insisted on buying him some large Scotches to warm up. At the end of the evening he escorted Father home (poor Father was obviously in a state of shock after his ordeal and kept buckling at the knees).

Sidney explained the whole situation to Mother, who had the frying-pan ready as soon as she heard Father's voice outside singing some rather rude songs. (The frying-pan was not to make his tea, which had long since been charred under the grill, but to make the point that she would rather Father had come home a little more in command of himself.)

Mother packed Father off to bed and poured Sidney some of her gin which she keeps for medicinal purposes. She was ever so grateful, she said, especially as the last premium on Father's life insurance appeared to have been overlooked.

Next day, my father could not praise Sidney highly enough. Not only had he saved his life once, he said, by pulling him out of the canal; he'd saved it a second time by persuading Mother to lay down the frying-pan. Greater love hath no man than this, especially twice, and he would be proud and honoured to have him in the family. After all, now that Sidney was a fully paid-up Slagville man, what possible objection could there be?

I was overjoyed. If Romeo had done something similar to Juliet's father, the play would have had a much happier ending. In fact, if Shakespeare were still alive, I'd write and suggest it; I'm sure it would make a better musical.

My rapture at all this has been overshadowed, however, by learning of Sidney's terrible Dark Secret. What I want to know is whether I should get Sidney to confess and take the consequences like a man; whether I should tell my parents at the risk of losing all; or whether I should keep it secret for all eternity as the only hope of saving our future happiness.

I met Sidney the next day in an ecstatic reunion and told him how much my parents and I admired his courage and daring, risking not only the perils of the canal, but also the frying-pan as he helped my father through the door. My father, especially, would be forever in his debt.

'That's good,' said Sidney. 'I only hope the old twit doesn't find out it was me who pushed him in.'

What *shall* I do?

Worried Blue Eyes

Dear Worried Blue Eyes,

Keep mum. Stay stumm. Breathe not a word. Let sleeping dogs lie. Let the end justify the means.

After all, what would be the result of confessing? Your father would once again go off Sidney, this time permanently. Not only that, he would possibly take his revenge at some future

91

date by pushing Sidney in the canal and, from the sound of your father, making sure he stayed there.

Desperate ills need desperate remedies, and Sidney did what he thought was best for your long-term future. Did, in other words, what a man had to do.

Not that it doesn't mean he's a cunning, unprincipled, Machiavellian little swine. But, there again, nobody's perfect.

King Conger

The 120lb conger hauled up in a trawler's net off Looe in Cornwall was certainly some catch. Nearly 10 feet long and as thick as a telegraph pole, making the British rod-caught record look like a Mothercare bootlace.

What do you do with a thing like that when it hits the deck? Apart from asking permission to leave the boat?

I'm as brave as the next man, providing the next man is Mad Mac, but I'm afraid my own reaction to a conger that size landing on the planks would be like Woody Allen's when he was asked if he was afraid of dying: 'No,' he said. 'I just don't want to be there when it happens.'

When the great Ernie Passmore caught a giant conger, as he did more often than the rest of us, he *stroked* it until it relaxed. But unless you're super-confident in your stroking ability, or don't mind being called Lefty for the rest of your natural, you might be better advised to use less subtle methods. Seems a bit mean, anyway, to stroke a conger until it's purring blissfully or giggling uncontrollably, and then to belt it one. Not really cricket.

One result of the capture of the 120-pounder was a new Jaws-type craze as anglers attempted to catch a similarly-sized fish on rod and line. Inevitably, a lot of smaller congers were caught and, just as inevitably, a lot of anglers were doing a lot of silly things with them. To the benefit of neither the conger nor the angler.

There's something about a conger that brings out the loony in the best-adjusted anglers, and part of the lunacy is the refusal to believe that a newly-clobbered conger is seldom as dead as it seems.

During a quiet spell, the proud captor often finds it impossible to resist poking about in his box of fish to locate the conger and admire it. Often the conger locates him first:

'Doctor – I've been bitten by a conger! Will I be able to play the violin after this?'

'Don't worry. It's not as bad as it looks. You'll be able to play the violin perfectly well.'

'That's funny. I never could before.'

It's even more dangerous, after a conger has been dropped in a sack, to feel around inside for it. Experienced conger fishermen always ask a mate to do it. It leads to some confusion in the pub later (and to ancient conger jokes such as this) when the angler shouts, 'Four pints, please!' and can only stick two fingers in the air.

But the prize loony is the one who hoiks the conger onto his knee, holds it by the back of the neck, and does a ventriloquist routine with it:

'And what's your name, little man?'

'Hidney.'

'Sidney, eh? That's a nice name. Would you like a bottle o' pop?'

'Hi'd hather hag a gottle o' geer.'

'Well you can't have a bottle of beer, Sidney. You're far too young. And look at me when I'm talking to you. Look into my eyes. Deep into my – Aaaarrrrgh!'

When the conger has been prised off his nose, does the former ventriloquist thank his mates for their efforts? Does he heck a like. He just sits there, glaring, and saying, 'I thuppothe you thig thad's bluddy fuddy!'

The jolly japes don't stop once the boat's docked, either. Then it's time for several anglers to take a conger apiece, tuck them head-to-tail under their arms so that they look like one incredibly long fish, and line up for a group photograph. The shot is often spoiled when one of the congers comes round and expresses its dislike of – or taste for – a smelly human armpit.

'Harold! Stop messing about! Just put that arm back on and say *Cheese* . . .'

Still, even an incident like that has its uses. At least it stops anyone volunteering for the most-congers-down-the-trousers record. So far that's one record which has never been claimed, most-down-the-trousers-record loonies preferring to stick to the old-fashioned ferrets.

Pub landlords fear the worst when a boatload of conger

fishermen arrives back. They know that before the night's over an affrighted maiden will rush screaming out of the Ladies because some wag has hung a conger on the back of the door. Or worse, stuck it in the loo pan with its head peering balefully from under the seat. And local police do get a bit fed up of untying the things from lamp posts. Does nobody ever take a conger home?

... The conger, by the way, is known in Scotland as 'Evil Eel'. If anybody wants to know why, just fish for it in a kilt.

There was a young lady . . .

Thought you'd like a bit of culture. A spot of uplifting poetry.

Not just ordinary poetry, either, but poetry with a message of deep social significance. Limericks, these are, all about the Angling Condition. The limerick, as you probably know, is so called because it didn't originate in Limerick. (It's best not to dwell on that too long.)

So here they come, courtesy of the Parker Foundation for Culture for the Masses.

* * *

The rise in the crime rate among anglers is causing some concern, especially among those who have had their gear nicked. But sometimes justice prevails:

> *A match fisherman from Devizes*
> *Ran away with all of the prizes.*
> *There was just one small snag:*
> *They fell out of the bag,*
> *And now he's awaiting Assizes.*

The increased cost of protective clothing is causing many underprivileged (i.e. skint) anglers to take chances with their health by going out inadequately dressed:

> *A poorly-clad angler from Widnes*
> *Got a terrible pain in his kidneys.*
> *His little short vest*
> *Didn't cover his chest*
> *And the long johns he wore were young Sidney's.*

Sometimes it is difficult to get the lines of a limerick to scan but in an issue as vital as the following, the content is much more important than the form, the message much more important than the medium:

An incautious young angler from Consett
Suffered one night from the onset
    Of frostbitten toes
    And Nightfisher's Nose
'Cos his clogs were being mended, his nose cosy
was at the cleaners, and of each he only had one set.

Mental and emotional stress is one thing. (Or possibly two things.) But physical danger is another. And in some branches of the sport the angler is risking life and limb, not to mention naughty bits:

A sea angler out of Torquay
Felt a terrible pain in his knee.
    He said, 'It's a conger!
    'I've never seen longer.
'I hope it's not stopping for tea.'

Obviously the physical danger is greatest in sea fishing, but it does not apply to that area exclusively:

A keen salmon angler from Melton
Went wading without any belt on.
    His very first cast
    Left his pants at half mast.
And he soon had a well-mended kelt on.

Cases of food poisoning are not uncommon in angling circles. Indeed, with the constant handling of maggots, worms, old sausage meat and chunks of salmonella-flavoured luncheon meat, it's a wonder there aren't many more:

A greedy young angler from Brum
Had a terrible pain in his tum.
    He said, 'Damn and blasters!
    'I've eaten me casters.
'I thought those last crisps tasted rum.'

But there are other ways of incapacitating oneself. And I must say that this one sounds more fun:

> *A night-fishing addict from Settle*
> *Was feeling on top of his mettle.*
> *To his tent dark and shady*
> *He took a young lady*
> *And now he's in no kind of fettle.*

Even an innocent day out on the river by the most skilled oarsman can end in disaster:

> *A loony old angler named Cliff*
> *Went fishing one day in a skiff.*
> *He was rammed by a lugger*
> *And the silly old person*
> *Went down with his skiff in a miff.*

But everything pales into insignificance compared to the fate of this poor lad. (Readers of a nervous disposition are warned, etc.):

> *An adventurous angler from Bray*
> *Took a slow boat to China one day.*
> *He was pinned to the tiller*
> *By a sex-starved gorilla.*
> *And China's a bloody long way . . .*

Thank you. And goodnight.

Monsters with everything

Every summer we run into the Silly Season. (What am I saying? The Silly Season in angling lasts for 365 days each year, except for leap years when it lasts for 366.)

The Silly Season for newspapers, however, runs through high summer, when people are too busy enjoying themselves to cause any hassle. Parliament is in recess, too, so there are no price-rise-shock-horror stories. The scribes really have to scratch around to fill the columns.

You can usually depend on a wolf-boy story from India or thereabouts. (That wolf-boy must be getting on a bit now. It's 35 years since I saw the story first, and it wasn't new then.) There's the regular Vicar-And-Gogo-Dancer-In-Lovenest-Drama, but not a lot else. Apart from the monsters.

Monsters, presumably, are there all the year round. So it's surprising how sightings tend to be made in summer just as editors are thinking they'll have to go to press with a hole on page one.

For at least three months a year you can't move on Loch Ness for all the people hounding poor old Nessie. They're taking pictures of ducks on top of the water and bits of rock underneath, and claiming that this time it's definitely the old girl herself.

Official odds against spotting Nessie in a twelve-month period are 100–1. They don't sound so bad until you consider that so far nobody's won. And even if Nessie is found, the bookies will only cough up if the thing is brought to London for examination. Try getting that in the back of the car.

Potty persons are still making bets in large amounts, and making handsome contributions to the Old Bookies' Home. One dedicated punter, presumably with more money than sense, lost £280,000 in one fell swoop.

Nessie's not the only monster being pursued. In Okanagan Lake in western Canada lives the Ogo Pogo Monster. (Eh, no. It's true is this.) For 300 years people living around the lake have been seeing the monster, some no doubt after over-indulgence in the local Mountain Dew. But there was the case of the perfectly sober teenage girl whose water-skis hit something on the lake. She came off, and under water found herself face to face with a reptilian beast about 40 feet long.

Something similar happened to a girl on a lake near where I live. The underwater creature wasn't quite so long, but it was still pretty repulsive: bloated body, pale leprous skin, walrus moustache, mad staring eyes. I said to Big McGinty afterwards: 'It was all your fault. You shouldn't have been swimming near the water-skiers in the first place.'

Enough of this flippancy. Back to the Ogo Pogo.

Yes, it frightened the girl so much that she refused to go back to the lake with a camera crew who were making a film about it.

In the old days, apparently, the monster used to annoy Indians and settlers by knocking off the horses swimming behind the boats. The settlers got so fed up with it that they used to put the horses in the boat and let their mothers-in-law swim behind. Then there were complaints from local animal protection societies about cruelty to monsters.

* * *

There were some monster fish in the Blue Nile, which I fished when I was in the Sudan, a-servin' of 'Er Majesty. (You've doubtless heard about Parker of the Nile, the Rambo of the Service Corps.) We never saw the biggest fish because they invariably broke the thick twine we used on the home-made palm-branch rods.

The two smallest blokes in the billet were a Geordie and a Scot, nicknamed Snitch and Snatch after Lord Snooty's little pals in the *Beano*. One day Snitch hooked one of the monsters. He held on tight to his rod and we all waited for the line to snap. It didn't. Instead, Snitch took off from the top of the bank in a graceful curve, landed in the river, and was towed out to midstream at a rate of knots.

'Let go, for God's sake!' yelled the lads on the bank, some out of concern for Snitch's safety, some out of plain jealousy, and some because he owed them a bob or two.

'Haway, man,' gurgled Snitch (you know how the Geordies talk). 'Ah've waited nearly two years for this. Ah'm havin' this bugger!'

'Could be a Nile Perch!' the lads shouted. 'Or a croc! It'll go for your wedding tackle!'

'Sod that!' yelled Snitch. 'Ah've only got six weeks to demob!'

So saying, he let go of the rod and churned back to the bank. The rod turned left in the middle of the river and headed upstream in the general direction of Ethiopia.

* * *

The nearest thing to a monster I've seen, apart from Big McGinty, was something which surfaced alongside the pier at Sandown, Isle of Wight. I don't know whether it was a basking shark or a whale, but there was a lot of it, all scarred and covered with weed and barnacles. It looked as if 30 feet of the bottom had suddenly decided to come to the top, and it certainly ruined the fishing for the lads lined up along the rails.

You've heard of British phlegm. The stolid courage of our island race, unflinching in the face of the most appalling dangers. There wasn't a lot of that about. Judging by the stampede to get away from The Thing, the pier must have been full of lily-livered foreigners. Either that, or 40 pressing previous engagements were suddenly remembered.

'Come back, you cowards!' I cried, shaking my fist at their retreating backs. Gad, Parker wasn't going to move for a little thing like a 30-foot monster. It would take more than that to scare me.

Besides which, I'd got my foot stuck in the railings.

A night to forget

Dear Uncle Clifford,

I now realise the full wisdom of your advice. I have said not a word to anyone, nor even confided the truth to my diary, as Mother has a habit of looking through it when I'm out.

As a result, the relationship between my father and Sidney has flourished. Gone from strength to strength, you might say. Mother, too, thinks the world of Sidney, even though her regard was temporarily clouded by the discovery that the premium on my father's life insurance policy had, in fact, been paid. We are now, the four of us, just one big, happy family.

So well is everybody getting on, in fact, that Sidney thought the time was ripe to take me nightfishing. He courteously asked my parents' permission, although strictly speaking he had no need to do so, me being of age for voting and whatever form of fishing I choose.

My father at first was dead against it. He was having no hanky-panky going on with his Little Girl, he said. He brushed aside Sidney's assurances about his motives being of the purest, and fishing the sole object of the expedition. He knew what went on in nightfishers' tents, my father said, having indulged in a spot of nightfishing with my mother during their courting days.

Mother, who I thought would have even stronger objections, was surprisingly in favour. I would come to no harm, she said, if Sidney hit the Scotch as hard as Father had on their outings. If my idea of fun was eight hours in a freezing cold tent listening to a comatose angler snoring the night away, then I was welcome to get on with it.

We got to the river at dusk. Sidney had chosen the river in preference to the canal as the bank offered better ground for pitching the tent than did the towpath. Apart from that, we would have a bit more privacy and wouldn't be disturbed by wandering drunks tripping over the tent in the dark.

Sidney's first act was to put up the tent. It was a great improvement on the one Father and Mother had used; I know because I used to play in theirs when I was little, and it was a squeeze for me even then. He hung up a battery-powered lamp inside, spread quilted sleeping-bags on the groundsheet, carried in a crate of assorted liquid refreshments and a portable radio, and then turned his attention to tackling up.

I must admit that the tackling up surprised me. My father had been muttering about the fact that mixed nightfishing never involved any actual tackle, the whole of the time being given over to hanky-panky and goings-on. But here was my Sidney giving the lie to such vile insinuations by setting up two rods, casting them out, and carefully fitting the electric buzzers which would give warning of a bite.

The preparations completed, Sidney invited me into the tent. Weren't we supposed to be sitting by the rods? I asked. No need, said Sidney. That's why he'd fitted the electric buzzers. Besides which, it would get cold outside. And besides which again, our presence on the bank would disturb the fish. If we wanted results, we had to stay inside the tent.

We sat on the sleeping-bags and, with the aid of a thermos flask, Sidney dispensed some hot toddies which I found quite warming. The radio was tuned to some soft music for night owls, which I found quite relaxing. 'But what about the results?' I asked. 'Shouldn't we be getting some soon?'

'Any minute now,' said Sidney. The lamp was the trouble, he said. Frightening away the fish, it was. So he turned it off, leaving the tent in complete darkness.

Over what happened next, I shall draw a veil, but Sidney certainly got results. A combination of the hot toddies, the fug in the tent and the soft music must have weakened my resolve, and I have to admit that a certain amount of hanky-panky and goings-on was indulged in. But, as Sidney said, if it could happen to Gary Cooper and Ingrid Bergman in *For Whom the Bell Tolls*, who were we to fight it? And as there had been no sound at all from the buzzers, he said, we might as well be doing something to pass the time.

Dawn broke in a beautiful romantic glow. Sidney went outside to reel in the rods, asking me to stay in the tent in case I caught a chill. But I felt in need of fresh air and followed him.

That was my biggest surprise of the outing.

I know that angling has its mysteries and its special techniques. But shouldn't there have been some bait on the hooks?

Worried Blue Eyes

Dear Worried Blue Eyes,

As any nightfisher will tell you, fish are often suspicious of bait during the hours of darkness, and will often prefer to take an unbaited hook. And Sidney's hooks may well have been baited originally. There are pike which are so cunning that they will stealthily nibble away at a whole herring until every last little bit has gone; carp which will suck a sweetcorn clean and spit out the skin; each without so much as a tremor on the line.

Any nightfisher will tell you.

Nightfishers being what they are.

The pinstripe-trousered philanthropist

'Get 'em off,' said Dearly Beloved.

'Get what off?' I asked.

'Your trousers.'

'This is no time for hanky-panky,' I said. 'I'm going fishing.'

'Not in those trousers, you're not.'

I had to admit that the trousers were a bit past their best. The sort that stand at ease when you're standing to attention. And they were a bit grubby with honorable stains of mud, weed, slime, groundbait; decorated here and there with fish scales and maggot skins. Every stain, every decoration, telling a stirring story.

The rip in the seat, sustained while negotiating some very tall barbed wire, was threatening at any minute to enlarge into something more spectacular. The faithful old things had seen better days.

But what had attracted Dearly Beloved's attention was the fly. Or rather, the lack of it. The zip had bust when I put the trousers on. There was no time, even if I'd had the skill, to fix the zip, so I'd done a temporary but neat repair job with a couple of safety-pins.

'Now look here,' I said. Asserting myself as Master of the Household. 'I'm the gaffer round here, and I say I'm going fishing. In these trousers. Got it?'

Five minutes later I was standing in the bedroom in my Snoopy Dog underpants, waiting for Dearly Beloved to bring my trousers back. I'd relented. Just to humour her, you understand. And she'd taken the trousers away for a quick zip operation. At least, that's what I thought.

She came back into the bedroom empty handed.

'Where are my trousers?' I aked.

'Here, put these on,' she said, pulling a pair of pinstripes from the wardrobe.

'Pinstripes?' I said.

'Yes. You never wear that suit these days. Not since your centre of gravity shifted. You may as well make use of the trousers. They're good enough for what you get up to.'

'I don't *want* flaming pinstripes! Who the hell goes fishing in pinstripes? I want my old trousers back! Where are they?'

Dearly Beloved pointed out of the window to the end of the garden where, from the incinerator, a cloud of trouser-coloured smoke was billowing.

'Aaarrrgh!' I cried. 'I'm ruined! Those were my lucky trousers!'

'They were lucky to have hung together all these years,' said Dearly Beloved. 'Wonder you've not been locked up. Now put these pinstripes on and let's have less. I'm going to start the decorating.'

At the mention of decorating, I immediately backed down. If I pushed my luck any further I might get roped in.

On with the trousers while Dearly Beloved went downstairs to get out the paint. Perhaps they wouldn't be so bad after a couple of trips. Bit of mud here, slime there, the odd splash of draught bitter, and you wouldn't notice the stripes at all.

Right. Downstairs. Collect tackle. Walk into front room for passionate Angler's Farewell to Dearly Beloved. Walk straight into four-inch paint brush with which Dearly Beloved is attacking the wall. Great big blob of paint goes *squidge* all over front of trousers.

'Egad!' I cried. 'You're not content with destroying my faithful old lucky trousers. You're now trying to tar and feather me!'

'Tar and feather be blowed,' said Dearly Beloved. 'Emulsion, that is. Wispy Peach. Very fetching. Tee-hee.'

I was faced with either giving up the day's fishing altogether, in the absence of any other suitably tatty trousers, or going in pinstripes with a smear of Wispy Peach all up the front.

With the threat of decorating hanging over me, pinstripes and Wispy Peach won, though I can't recommend them. You don't half get some funny looks.

By the water was ol' buddy Mad Mac. Some buddy.

'Taken up banking, I see,' he said. 'And painting, by the look of it. Does that mean your account's in the pink?'

'I'll have you know that is *not* pink,' I said. 'Wispy Peach, that is.'

'Wispy Peach? Ooh, ducky . . .'

'Shurrup.'

* * *

Came the time of the morning when the fish stop biting, i.e. opening time.

'Er, a subject of some delicacy,' said Mac. 'I'm skint. Can you stake me to a pint or two? Three, perhaps? I'll see you right next week.'

'It just so happens you're in luck,' I said. 'I have about my person a fiver with which I was supposed to pay the milkman yesterday. Unfortunately he missed me. Possibly because I was hiding behind the settee.'

'Good thinking,' said Mac. 'OK then, philanthropic ol' buddy, let's go.'

In the pub, two pints of foaming best pulled and placed on the bar by large landlord. Hand into back pocket for fiver which, but for my initiative and resource, would now be swelling the coffers of Express Dairies.

Hand out of back pocket. Hands into side pockets. Hands into anorak pockets.

Eek! The fiver!

It was in the back pocket of my lucky trousers. And is now part of a pile of ash in the incinerator.

'Er . . . landlord. A subject of some delicacy . . .'

Large landlord looms. Largely.

Just wait till I get home. I'll give her Wispy Peach . . .

Doing what comes naturally

Some anglers swear by natural baits, but I've never had much luck with them.

Last autumn I collected a couple of sacksful of elderberries. Most of them were to be turned into elderberry wine, courtesy of a lethal recipe supplied by Cousin Jim from Leeds ('Elder-burbleberry' you're calling it after a couple of stiff ones), but the rest were to be used as bait.

I stuck them in the room laughingly called my study (when you can get in it for the ironing-board, vacuum-cleaner and things).

When Dearly Beloved got back from the shops I couldn't wait to show her what I'd collected.

'There,' I said, throwing open the door. 'What do you think of –?'

'Eek!' she screamed.

'What's up?' I said.

'Look!' she said.

'Eek!' I screamed.

Earwigs.

The floor, walls and ceiling were alive with earwigs. Hundreds and hundreds of the things. They must have been hidden deep within the bunches of elderberries.

'Have no fear,' I said, taking instant command of the situation. 'I'll get a dustpan and brush. They'll make super bait.'

'Oh, no they won't!' expostulated Dearly Beloved, still giving vent to the occasional *Eek!* (Expostulated. That's a good 'un. Must use it again some time.) 'You'll get the creepy-crawly killer and spray that room. I'm not letting you out until every last one is stiffened.'

Any idea how long it takes to stiffen a roomful of ear-wigs?

While all the screaming was going on, Daft Cat shot out of the room in a state of abject terror. She's never been right in the head since jumping on a hedgehog as a kitten, but being covered in earwigs did nothing to improve her state of mind.

* * *

Caterpillars I do pretty well for, my veg. patch being in the nature of a caterpillar sanctuary. But even the innocent looking caterpillar can be dangerous. I found an enormous green one, stuffed to bursting with cabbage. When I picked it up, that's just what the damn thing did. Burst.

It exploded and left me with a shirt-front covered in fermenting cabbage and bits of shredded caterpillar. Fermenting cabbage and bits of shredded caterpillar do not smell very nice.

Slugs I also do pretty well for, having a garden with the highest slug-population density west of the Pecos. But I've never had much success with them as bait: at least not with the small ones and I can't bring myself to use the big ones.

Ever looked closely at a slug? They're really beautiful – especially the orange ones – delicately made, little eyes waving

about on stalks. Highly vulnerable and at the mercy of all sorts of slug-eating creatures.

When I come across a huge grandad slug – or grandma, for all I know: slugs are very difficult to sex – I realise how long it must have taken to get to that size, and all the perils it must have survived. After all that I'm not going to spoil it by sticking a hook in it and drowning the poor old thing.

My mate Mitch gets plenty of slugs by putting down bowls of beer on his allotment. I could get plenty this way myself, but resent parting with a can of wallop which I can put to far better use.

And Mitch did have his tragedy. Floating in the beer one morning was a little mouse. Dead as a doornail, but looking ever so pleased with itself. It had obviously died happy.

Mitch and his mate Fred gave it a decent burial. Laid it reverently under the sod and said a few words over it. Neither of them had the script for the burial service about his person, but they made do by reciting the tide tables for the Isle of Wight.

Incidentally, for anyone thinking of catching slugs like this, but mindful of the well-being of little alcoholic mice, there is a gadget on the market called the Slug Pub. It is filled with beer and lets the slugs in, but nothing bigger. The dead slugs are lifted out in a sort of colander, which enables the beer to be used again.

I've had no reports on the effect of beer-sodden slugs on the fish, but no doubt there are gudgeon lurching about saying, 'I'll fight any pike in this canal, so I will! So you think you're tough, eh? Put 'em up! Put 'em up . . .!'

Where is thy sting?

Dear Uncle Clifford,

I'm afraid that relations between Sidney and my father have become a little strained again.

Father was suspicious, for a start, about our nightfishing expedition. Even though I did not mention the absence of bait, the fact that Sidney had not even had a buzz, let alone a fish, caused him to shoot some very old-fashioned glances in my beloved's direction.

Thankfully, something turned up to take Father's mind off it. A wasps' nest, it was, built inside our loft. Father was poking around up there, muttering something about a horsewhip, when he came across the nest under the eaves.

'Marvellous!' he said when he came down, the horsewhip apparently forgotten. 'Fantastic bait, wasp grubs. And there's enough there to see me in free pints for a month if I take them along to the club. The only problem is, how do we get 'em down?'

Sidney, who is of a serious and scientific turn of mind, said that he had read somewhere that in autumn the wasps' nest discipline begins to break down. The worker wasps, which are the ones with the stings, are gorging themselves on overripe fruit. This results in a state of intoxication which causes them to abandon their duties of tending the grubs and become disinclined to sting anybody. The male wasps, as opposed to the workers, are stingless anyway, so there should be no trouble at all in removing the nest unscathed.

Sidney advised against using an agricultural-strength wasp killer because in a confined space it could prove fatal to the user.

'Let him get on with it,' said Mother, less concerned about

112

Father's survival now that she knew the life insurance premium was paid.

No, said Sidney. He would get an aerosol tin of insect killer, which should be quite strong enough at least to stun the wasps, and which even then was perhaps an unnecessary precaution. The plan was that he would spray the nest, Father would wrench it from under the eaves, and they could dismantle it at their leisure in the garage.

Mother and I heard the first couple of squirts of the aerosol in the loft, and a sound like tearing paper as Father pulled the nest clear. Then there followed the most blood-curdling screams.

Sidney scrambled down the loft ladder, squirting his aerosol frantically into space, and ran outside. Father stumbled down next, with a great cloud of angry wasps buzzing around his head, leapt in great bounds down the back garden and dived head first into the water butt.

Mother and I ran out of the house through the front door, slamming it behind us, and took refuge with the Higginsons across the road, from where we rang up the council's emergency pest control service. Luckily, there was a pest officer free; he was round in ten minutes and, in suitable protective clothing, sprayed the whole house from loft to kitchen.

Only then dared Mother and I go in search of Father and Sidney. We found Sidney lying prostrate on the back lawn, with Father giving him some quite severe kicks in the ribs with the toe of his boot. Both were covered in angry lumps, Father more so than Sidney, and even the poor cat was coming out in the odd one.

Mother pulled Father away and told him that the wasp stings would be good for his rheumatism. Or was it bees? Anyway, he'd no call to treat the poor lad like that when all he'd done was try to help.

What I want to know is where did Sidney go wrong? It's not like him to make a mistake.

Worried Blue Eyes

Dear Worried Blue Eyes,

Sidney certainly didn't go wrong with the first rule of wasp-grub collecting, which is: Let somebody else get 'em. As squirt operative he had a better chance of getting away than did your father, who was left holding the babies.

Where Sidney went wrong was in assuming that *all* the worker wasps would be sloshed and stingless. There are usually some with enough sense of responsibility to stay off the booze. Even so, the breakdown of nest discipline often doesn't happen until after the first frosts. A mild autumn could mean wasps in a nasty mood until quite late.

It may be some consolation to your father that his present painful condition could act as an antidote to wasp stings, should he get any more this year. Somehow, I don't think he will.

For the angler who has everything

Executive toys are the things in the corridors of power. Or so it seems.

'Be the first on your board to pull out your executive yo-yo!' said the ad in a business paper. 'Delight your colleagues!!! Baffle your rivals!!! Amaze your boss!!!'

Ever heard anything so daft? Toys for grown-ups. And executives at that. American, of course. Only the Yanks could think up something so totally useless.

But a little later what did I find? That a British firm is making a steady bob or two out of executive toys. Giant matches, with giant matchboxes. Newton's Cradle, which is basically all balls, proving the laws of inertia or some such in boardrooms all over the country. Magnetic decision-makers to remove the danger of brain fag. Mindbender puzzles to put the brain fag back. All selling like stink.

By gum, I thought. These lads aren't so daft after all. And here's Parker's chance to cash in and retire to an island in the sun. Or Blackpool. With his exclusive range of Loonigear – the prezzies for the angler who has everything.

Some of them, the real prestige jobs, are totally, absolutely and completely useless. Just like the executive toys. These include the Rubber Rod Rests, Balsa Leger Weights and Fast-sink Floats. Not to mention the Cast-iron Swingtips, the Knitted Quivertips and the Hookless Barbs.

The Fair Weather Umbrella is pretty useless, too. It's a really massive job with nine-foot spokes. No canopy, just nine-foot spokes.

The Dead Livebait is having a little difficulty in getting off the ground. I'm working on a Live Deadbait, but there are certain technical difficulties still to be overcome.

The Lead-lined Basket is completely waterproof, but its real appeal is to the angler who isn't going anywhere: the lining weighs three hundredweight.

Very spectacular are the Flying Fish Plugs. Every time you

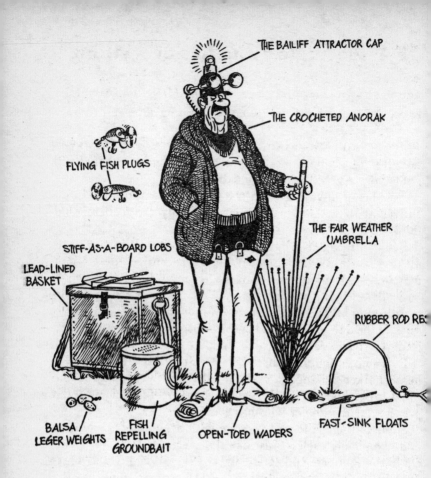

THE BAILIFF ATTRACTOR CAP

THE CROCHETED ANORAK

FLYING FISH PLUGS

THE FAIR WEATHER
UMBRELLA

STIFF-AS-A-BOARD LOBS

LEAD-LINED
BASKET

RUBBER ROD RES

BALSA
LEGER WEIGHTS

FISH
REPELLING
GROUNDBAIT

OPEN-TOED WADERS

FAST-SINK FLOATS

wind them in they jump three feet out of the water. Nothing like them for livening up a dreary day's spinning. There have been complaints from the RSPCA, however, that their prolonged use can send pike potty and cause damage to low-flying ducks.

Then there are the useful prezzies.

The Open-toed Waders, for instance, are an infallible guide to the depth of water. The Crocheted Anorak makes sure you get all the benefit of God's good air and the softly falling rain.

Both the Non-opening Bait Dropper and the Unperforated Block-end Swimfeeder ensure an incredible saving on the cost of maggots. Once they're in, they can't get out, and one filling lasts all day.

The Twelve-inch Mesh Keep Net and Landing Net are for the really ambitious specimen hunter, or for the dozy angler who doesn't want the bother of putting his fish back at the end of the session.

The Ready-gunjed Reel has a mechanism already choked with damp sand. This saves you having to drop it on the bank to get the same effect.

The Stiff-as-a-board Lobs come tastefully packed in boxes of six. These are lobworms which have been fed on a special diet: three of sand and one of cement. Not a wriggle between the lot. They don't catch fish but they do last for ever. And the panatella-sized pack fits comfortably into the breast pocket.

The Fish-repelling Groundbait and No-hope Hookbait mean that you can spend all the time in the pub, safe in the knowledge that there's no chance of a bite.

And if you're ever in the agonising position of having to decide whether to fish on in a blizzard or go for a pint, there's the Parker Decision-maker: a solid brass double-headed penny. It comes complete with instructions: *Heads is Pub*.

A very sophisticated toy is the Freshwater Finger Mincer, which imparts an authentic impression of a set of pike's choppers. Makes you an instant wounded hero in the pub and saves you all that messing about with gags and disgorgers. There are sea-fishing versions, too, which simulate damage from shark, conger, ling or whiting (state preference when ordering).

For those who like to live dangerously, there's the Bailiff Attractor, a cap fitted with a flashing light and a hooter which blows a raspberry every five seconds. When the bailiff comes thundering over, you can greet him with a disarming smile and produce your All-purpose, All-water Season Ticket. It is inscribed very simply, in beautiful copperplate: 'This bloke is a bum. Book him.'

Those reticent souls who don't really like playing hell when somebody has nicked their pre-baited swim or is fishing too close, may like to try the Instant Insult Kit. This is a high-powered tape recorder which booms out, 'Hey, you! Yes, you! Cloth Ears! Get out of my swim, you bulbous-nosed, bandy-legged, pin-brained heap! Or I'll come over there and treat you to a knuckle butty! Tear your arms off and knot 'em round your neck! Tear your legs off and stick your wellies up your nose! Make you late for your mother's wedding!'

If the bloke turns out to be bigger than you thought, not to worry. There's the Parker First Aid Kit, complete with splints, oxygen cylinder and bankside traction tackle. This really *is* for the angler who has everything – concussion, dislocated shoulder, stove-in ribs, broken leg . . .

Brothers under the skin

I am not among those who, in defence of angling, are also prepared willy-nilly to defend such goings-on as foxhunting. It'll give us a bad name, that kind of thing.

But ever since angling found itself in a defensive alliance with hunting, it has been essential for those in the two areas of activity to be able to recognize each other: contact in the normal course of events being rare, brief and often acrimonious.

It is easy enough for the angler to recognise the hunting fraternity. They're the ones in shiny boots and loud jackets who gather on large horses outside boozers which are not yet open, but whose landlord is honoured to serve them with the traditional stirrup cup.

After passing the hat among the assembled peasantry to help support them in the way to which they are accustomed, they trot off in the company of a bunch of large and noisy dogs. The idea is to reach open country and eventually pick up the scent of a fox. Their progress is sometimes retarded by the dogs' taking a short cut through a council estate or caravan site and doing nasty things to the odd cat.

With the late cat's owner soundly thrashed for kicking the dogs, the hunt carries on until it finds a fox.

The dogs are bred for stamina, not for speed. Which means they don't catch up with the fox until it is absolutely clapped out, providing the hunt with an extended romp over carefully tended and heavily subsidised farmland.

When they do catch up, the dogs do things to the fox which hurt more than somewhat. It is not a good way to go.

Blood from the defunct creature is rubbed on the faces of infants who all their young lives have been carefully protected from video nasties. Bits of it are then chopped off and presented to consenting adults, in time-honoured ceremonies rooted in our grand old sporting traditions.

* * *

It is much more difficult for a huntsman to recognise an angler, the angler on the whole being quieter, less conspicuous and seldom moving in the same social circles.

Here we call on the expert knowledge of Sir Humphrey Tramplingham-Downe, MFH, one of the few huntsmen to have come across an angler in his natural habitat. The following is the text of his address to the All-British Killing Things Co-ordinating Committee:

'It has been suggested that huntsmen would not know an angler if they fell over one. I'm here today to tell you that this is absolute poppycock. I fell over one the other day, or at least my horse did, and I recognised the bounder almost immediately.

'Skulking in the undergrowth, he was, camouflaged to the eyeballs. How is a horse to avoid stepping on the blighters when they insist on lurking about like ill-clad Japanese snipers?

'He took it all very badly, I must say: hopping around, clutching his broken leg and uttering the most dreadful oaths. I was about to take my crop to him, to stop him spooking old Trumper, when I realised he must be one of those angler chaps we're supposed to be fraternising with.

'I threw him one of those £1 chocolate coins, told him to hop along and get his leg attended to, and all I got for my pains was a stream of abuse.

'Adversity makes strange bedfellows, however, and we have to cultivate the friendship of these oiks. Hearts and Minds and all that. And the first step is to identify the blighters.

'I'm talking about coarse anglers, naturally, which just about sums them up. Game fishermen are more our sort and often quite respectable-looking. Even knew a chap whose sister married one.

'The coarse angler is quite a different kettle of fish. In fact he looks more like a mess of pottage. Smells like a drain, too, as you'd expect from the Great Unwashed.

'He's almost impossible to spot in the undergrowth, but when he emerges he's unmistakable. Incredibly scruffily dressed, and smeared all over with mud, slime, maggot skins and bits of cheese and pickle. He's got up like a Christmas tree with all sorts of baskets and cans and rods and things and sometimes carries a golfing umbrella, which I think is a bit of a nerve.

'He's generally unshaven, which gives you some idea of the type we're dealing with, often has a few teeth missing, and doesn't even speak the Queen's English. Obviously didn't go to a good school.

'He is excruciatingly ill mannered, not to say anti-social. A typical over-sensitive, lily-livered product of the Welfare State. Gets the odd horse stepping on his tackle, a few hounds eating his sandwiches and groundbait, perhaps taking the odd playful nip at his leg, and he goes absolutely berserk. Chip on the shoulder, if you ask me.

'Thankfully, even in this day and age, we can still keep our distance. The coarse angler tends not to use the same hostelry as the local hunt, thanks mainly to the good taste of the landlord.

'And in spite of our heartfelt desire for closer association, we must on no account allow them in. Let them stand in the yard with the hunt servants, by all means, and we can pass out the odd bottle of brown ale to deserving cases, but there it must stop. *Noblesse oblige*, and all that, but we do have standards to uphold.

'In conclusion, all I can say is, "Take heart". Our time will come. When it does, we can put these bounders well and truly back in their place. Get 'em off decent hunting land and back on the canal where they belong.

'There are no Gentlemen of the Press here, are there? Just as well. You can't trust any of those swine, either . . .'

Putting it where it's at

High-protein baits may be sure-fire fish attractors, but they don't come cheap. And they get dearer by the season.

It's not so much the hook baits that cost the money (for the number of bites I get, two or three flash-fried hi-protein black-pudding balls will last all day). No, it's the groundbait. A few handful of that and the old *après-pêche** social fund (i.e. beer money) is looking a bit sick.

I've always been heavy on groundbait because of my general lack of accuracy. I tend to depend on the splatter effect, being a bit short-sighted, unco-ordinated and not over-endowed with means of propulsion such as muscles. (When I was at school they stopped me putting the shot; every time I got the damn thing up to my shoulder I fell flat on my back. Never happened to Geoff Capes.)

But I can't go on just throwing bait out and hoping for the best. I'm practising accuracy and investigating the means of getting just the right amount in exactly the right places.

An old angling book I've got suggests swimming out with the groundbait. That must have been written when Britain was a tropical swamp; these days it's a bit chilly round the Trossachs.

And you could swim out, drop the bait, swim back to the board that says NO FISHING, and find the bailiff writing underneath: AND NO SWIMMING, NEITHER. What if he confiscated your clothes, leaving you to get back home starkers?

I can hear the wife now: 'You didn't walk all the way home like that, did you?'

'No, love. I caught the bus.'

If I've actually to take the stuff out to the fish, I'd prefer to use a boat. For future reference I can always put a chalk mark

---

* *Après-pêche*. French, that is, for after fishing. Like, when you're boozing after ski-ing, it's *après-piste*. They said it, not me.

on the side to show where I've dropped the bait. The danger here is that somebody might rub the chalk mark off, or I might not get the same boat next time out. (End of Irish groundbait jokes.)

There's the old-fashioned angler's throwing stick, of course; either thick bamboo with the top joint sliced vertically in half, or an ordinary stick with a dessert spoon tied to the top. I find the bamboo type OK for distance, but a bit lacking in accuracy. With the other, I find that after a few throws the spoon tends to come off and follow the bait. The wife is getting a bit fed up of eating custard with a fork.

I did think of catapults, especially after I discovered one with a pistol grip, arm support, wrist guard and other aids to accuracy and distance. But I had one or two reservations, apart from the fact that I did myself a mischief just pulling the elastic to full stretch. A catapult is too much of a temptation when there are intrusions in your swim, such as swans, ducks, power boats, and little lads throwing bricks from the opposite bank.

'What did you get today, darling?'

'Oh, a couple of roach, two ducks, a swan, a feller with a commodore's cap and a snotty-nosed little tyke who was fishing too close.'

At one point I thought I'd really found the answer: a giant pea-shooter. You can get them in plastic, about three feet long and with a half-inch bore. Saw a bloke using one. He filled it with small balls of bait, rolled in flour to reduce friction, and blew them a hell of a distance.

It looked highly impressive and completely foolproof. Until his mate came along, just as the lad was about to blow, grabbed hold of the other end and blew first.

With mates like mine, I daren't risk it. There's something about flour-coated minced worm-and-catfood balls that puts you off your ale. Even if they are flash-fried.

Finally I thought of a kite, with a little platform underneath that could be tilted when it was over the target. But for that you need a smooth lift-off if you're not going to be covered in protein and have tweety-birds pecking at you the rest of the day. And you need the wind blowing steadily in the right direction.

It could be embarrassing, after a sudden crosswise gust, to have a police person striding down the bank towards you. Blowing black-pudding balls out of his walkie-talkie.

''Ello, 'ello, 'ello. Having a nice play are we? And what little toys have we here, then?'

'Nothing officer. Ha ha. Just a kite, a throwing stick, a catapult and a pea-shooter.'

I've heard that the best job is in the prison library.

A breath of fresh air

Dear Uncle Clifford,

All was well that ended well after the Great Wasps' Nest Disaster. Though Father was more badly stung than Sidney, he recovered much faster. Mother reckons that it would take a meat cleaver to get through his thick hide, let alone a wasp.

His recovery was perhaps speeded by the fact that the pest officer presented him with the nest, which was absolutely crammed with grubs. Father lost no time in packing the grubs into empty yogurt cartons and rushing down to the club to trade them in for pints.

Poor Sidney seemed to be allergic to the few stings he had and went down very badly. His bruised ribs couldn't have helped, either.

'Serve the silly little sod right,' said my father, which I thought was a bit callous and unfeeling, especially as he hadn't saved a single grub for my beloved.

However, it did put Father in a better mood and ready to shake hands when Sidney finally rose from his bed of pain and sickness.

November came in cold and windy, and Sidney was disinclined to go fishing, being reluctant to expose his enfeebled frame to the elements.

'Rubbish,' said my father. 'Do you the world of good. Blow the cobwebs off. Why, when I was your age . . .'

He rabbited on a bit about National Service and things, and then suggested they went spinning for pike. He and Sidney would be on the move, he said, taking healthy exercise as they went. Just the thing to get the little wimp back on his knees, he said, and put the pallor back in his cheeks.

Father suggested the flash behind the plastics factory. This brought no protests from Sidney, as fishing the flash was one of the reasons he'd joined Slagville Piscatorials. So, early one Saturday morning, off they set.

Mother and I were not too concerned when, by ten o'clock that night, they had not arrived home. Such time-keeping is not rare in angling circles. By 11.30 we were beginning to get just a little bit worried. But by midnight our fears were proved groundless by a phone call. Father and Sidney were fine, said the caller, who identified himself as the Piscatorials' secretary. Nothing to worry about. All we had to do was collect them.

'Collect them?' said Mother. 'Where from?'

'Sludgethorpe General Infirmary. Casualty ward.'

. . . It was Father's fault, according to Sidney. The silly old (and I quote) bugger had taken him to that god-forsaken hole of a flash, across which a Force Nine gale was blowing, and insisted on casting into the wind. This resulted a couple of times in Father's spinner making contact with Sidney's left ear, resulting in severe pain for Sidney and some bad language from Father who told him to stop screaming like a bloody great wet nelly, get the hooks out and stop holding up the fishing.

. . . It was Sidney's fault, according to Father. Fishing too close to him, for a start. Not having the sense to duck, for a second. And carrying on like that. He had another ear, for God's sake.

It was Sidney's fault, too, that Father had fallen in, said Father. Fishing too close again, the daft little sod. Causing Father to glance sideways on the backswing and miss his footing on the bank. Either that or he was pushed. Always did have his doubts about that incident on the canal.

Both agreed, however, on packing up and going back to the club to dry out and take a little something to ease the pain and warm them through. Which caused them, on their return to the water after the bar had closed, to lose a little of their caution.

Darkness was falling and they were both about to give up when Sidney hooked a large pike. Pure skill, he said. Pure bloody fluke, said Father. This time Sidney fell in as he wrestled the creature towards the bank. It was left to Father to snatch the rod from him as he tumbled, and to net the thing just as Sidney was scrambling out.

Both of them fell on the pike, each claiming the fish as his own, and both insisted on taking the hooks out. They both had fingers inside as the pike closed its mouth.

They took the pike back between them to the club to show the other members. The fish arrived there six inches longer than it was at the moment of capture, which Father and Sidney put down to the fantastic growth rate of pike, but which others put down to all the pulling and tugging which went on.

From what we've been able to gather since, the two of them spent the whole evening at the bar, drinking left-handed with severe blood poisoning setting in in their respective right hands, and alternately boasting and squabbling.

Towards closing time, things were getting really heated and on the point of being settled by a bout of fisticuffs. But just as both drew their left hands back, they collapsed from a combination of hypothermia, incipient septicaemia and severe alcohol poisoning.

Uncle Clifford, is this any way for two mature men to carry on? Is there any hope that their relationship will settle down into something less volatile? Surely all anglers don't behave like this?

Worried Blue Eyes

Dear Worried Blue Eyes,

This is certainly no way for two mature men to carry on, but angling imparts to its practitioners a certain Peter Pan quality. They don't mature; they just get older.

All anglers certainly don't behave like this. Only about 93.5 per cent of them do; the other 6.5 per cent are women.

The relationship between your father and Sidney should sort itself out next month at the club's Christmas social. Nothing like the festive season for spreading comfort and joy and goodwill to all men. Just you wait and see . . .

Hearts and Glowers

There are a lot of instances, in these days of high unemployment, of role-reversal. The wife goes out to work and the husband stays at home to cook and clean and look after the house. This has led in some cases to the women insisting on privileges formerly reserved for men, and to men putting up with the drudgery and restrictions formerly reserved for women.

Let's hope it doesn't spread too far. Consider what would happen if the women went out fishing and the blokes were left at home. If the women behaved like we behave.

There you'd be, the dedicated house-husband, sitting up late in your dressing-gown and curlers, tapping your foot and muttering:

'Where the hell can she be until this time? Her tea's burnt to a cinder with me keeping putting it back under the grill. I hope she's not going to come out with the same lame excuse: that she met some of the girls on the way back from the canal, they stopped off at a pub for a quick one, and before she knew it it was past closing time.

'Let's hope she's in better condition than she was last week. Brought to the door by a policeman. Found talking to a tomcat at the end of the road, she was. Oh, the shame of it. Then covering the policeman with kisses and telling him he looked like Robert Redford. This Redford feller must look a lot like King Kong, that's all I can say.

'Let's hope her wellies are clean, too. The stuff she brought back on them last time! And trod it all over my new lounge carpet. She can leave that smelly old tackle in the garage, as well. I'm not having it festooning every room and stinking the place out. And those maggots are definitely *not* going back in the fridge.

'She's not wearing that lucky bra again, either, before it's been tubbed. Damn disgrace, it is. I wouldn't care, but it's nowhere near a fit after all these years. She can't realise that she's not the slim young thing she was when she won the club Krypton Factor championship in 1973.

'Mind you, it's not so bad when she comes home on her own. It's when she brings all her boozy mates back that the trouble really starts. That Ethel Droopidrorse ought to be locked up. Two Babychams and she's anybody's. Just can't keep her hands to herself.

'And that Olive Chuggalug! Talk about *sup*. If I hadn't produced that bottle of Scotch I keep for my chest, she'd have finished off all my metal polish.

'And eat! Eat me out of house and home, the wife's mates do. Like a bunch of flaming termites. Bunty Rumbold scoffed a pound and a half of biscuits and then started looking round for something else. Don't wonder the cat hid in the airing cupboard.

'The noise they make, too. Alice Chuckerbutty's got a voice like a foghorn and she will *not* keep it down. Singing all those rude songs at three in the morning. I don't wonder Mister Nextdoor got a petition up. I'd have signed it myself if I'd been asked. How I faced the lads at the Sewing Circle next day, I'll never know.

'Then having to come down in the morning to find them sprawled all over my new three-piece suite and the place littered with empty bottles. Not to mention the dead pike they leave all over the floor. Mind you, even that's better than finding the pike stuffed down the back of the settee three weeks later.

'And all this nightfishing worries me. Out in that tent all night, sometimes for two and three nights at a time. It wouldn't be so bad if I thought she was just fishing. But when I find a bloke's sock among the tent pegs . . . well, what *am* I supposed to think?

'What was that? Yes, it's her all right. Singing *I've Got a Lovely Bunch of Coconuts* at the top of her voice. She'll have the whole neighbourhood up. There goes the garden gate. Sounds as if she's fallen over it. Again. Footsteps lurching up the path. Oh, she's had a few tonight all right. Crash! There go the milk bottles. Now she's fallen over the cat. Better get her inside before she does any more damage.

'Come in, you! This minute! And stop kicking that cat! I don't know what Mister Nextdoor's going to say in the

129

morning. There'll be another petition round before we know it. *And* complaints to the council.

'Where the hell do you think you've been till now? If you think I'm going to sit here night after night, watching your tea burn to a frazzle, you've got another think coming. Father was right about you. Not the full shilling, he said. And a booze artist with it.

'What? Don't you dare say that about my father! It's a pity I didn't listen to him when I had the chance. Now get inside! And get those wellies off before you put one foot over that step!'

* * *

Yes, if the little women behaved as we do, we'd certainly have something to put up with.

Turns you cold, doesn't it?

I'm shy, Mary Ellen, I'm shy

I'm shy, that's my trouble.

Been like it ever since I was born, when my mother said, 'Very funny. The joke's over – now show me the baby.'

As a youth I was very skinny, and that didn't help. I used to get sand kicked in my face by seven-stone weaklings. Charles Atlas sent me my money back.

When I went for my National Service medical, I walked in wearing just my trousers clutched round my waist.

'Drop 'em,' said the doc. I dropped 'em. He turned pale.

'Has it finally come to this?' he said. 'Who sent you? The enemy?'

A few years ago I thought I'd got over it. Become a sophisticated man of the world, I had. Put on weight. Very big in Eccles. Then I was offered as a prize by an angling paper.

'Fish with the superstars,' it told its readers. 'Winners of this competition will be taken for a day's fishing with the country's top anglers. Just name your fishing superstar' – and there was my name among the greats – 'and he's all yours.'

By gum, I'd made it. No more shyness for me. I didn't care if people *did* call me Bighead.

When the competition results were announced, I was the only one nobody claimed. Set me back years, that did. It was six months before I stopped sulking and agreed to eat my greens again.

* * *

Mad Mac is shy as well. At his National Service medical he was so embarrassed that he forgot his name. Had to look in his wallet to find out who he was.

At a party once he was introduced to a topless girl. Actually, she had an excellent top, but there was nowt over it. He went to shake hands, missed, and shook her by something completely different. Confusion brought about by shyness, you see. At least, that's his story.

So there were Mac and I on the bank, talking about this shyness thing. According to a psychologist in the paper, there's a lot of it about, and they're even opening special National Health clinics to treat it. They're not doing all that well, because people are too shy to go.

There's certainly a disproportionate amount of shyness among anglers. Indeed, the sport is tailor-made for the retiring types who can't cope with people but get on quite well with gudgeon. Club life helps the condition up to a point, but anglers still spend too much time alone, talking to trees and occasionally getting taken away for it.

Another snag is that the shyness is compounded by the hostility encountered by the angler in public places and conveyances. In pubs he is told to stop steaming in front of the fire.

Or to stand in the yard with those muddy wellies. Or asked which scarecrow he pinched his outfit from.

Toffee-nosed chinless twits ask what kind of a fisherman he is. When he replies, 'Coarse,' they say nasty things such as, 'That's putting it mildly, old boy. Haw haw.'

He is often thrown off buses by the conductor for attempting to board in that condition and with all that gear. If he does get on, he gets black looks from well-dressed matrons, or causes heart attacks among little old ladies who think he's a hijacker.

... Mac and I walked back from the water wearing our superbly-cut Oxfam fishing outfits. From a house nearby came a very angry lady person.

'I've had enough!' she shouted. 'This time I'm going to complain to the council. Every time you empty my bin you leave a trail of rubbish all down the path!'

Enough to give anybody a complex.

* * *

Safe in the pub, I showed Mac the bit in the paper where the psychologist said that symptoms of shyness were laughing nervously, smoking like a chimney and drinking as if there were no tomorrow.

'By heck,' said Mac, lighting a fag, taking a swig from his pint and laughing nervously. 'I've met people like that.'

'What you have to do to overcome it,' I said, 'is smile. That's what this psychologist recommends.'

'Like this?' said Mac, coming out with a leer which stopped the clock.

'My God, no. You've got to do it properly.'

'I've not smiled much,' said Mac, 'since I lost my two front teeth at that disputed weigh-in.'

'Well you'll just have to persevere. What you do, it says here, is to give facial signals which will endear you to others:

'One. Look the other person straight in the eyes.

'Two. Begin by pouting, with your mouth turned down.

'Three. Gradually curve your mouth upwards, silently counting to ten, until it is as wide as it will go.

'Got it? Right. It's your round. Go and try the smile on the landlord. Might make him crack *his* face for a change.'

Mac went up to the bar, looked the landlord straight in the eyes, pouted, then came out with a big beaming smile to the count of ten. A bit lacking on the teeth, I thought, but certainly guaranteed to endear him to the stoniest heart.

He came back empty-handed.

'What's up?' I asked.

'He won't serve us. Says he doesn't want our sort in here. Would we kindly go and pout somewhere else.'

* * *

So that's one technique we are certainly not using to overcome our shyness and endear us to bailiffs and match stewards. Can you imagine the headlines: ANGLING SUPERSTARS BANNED FOR POUTING.

These days it's strictly teeth clenched and lips zipped.

Mind you, I am getting a bit fed up of going into pubs and asking for a Gint of Gitter and a Gottle of Guinness.

Better than pouting, though – whatever the psychologist says.

Home, James

'I don't know,' said Dearly Beloved to Darling Daughter. 'What *are* we going to do with him?'

Just because I'd fallen asleep on the last train home, was unnoticed by the guard, possibly because of my recumbent posture (I appear to have slid down under the seat), and was shunted into the sidings for the night.

I blame it on the full moon. Always has a strange effect on me.

'Full moon, rubbish,' said Dearly Beloved, toying nervously with her garlic necklace. 'Now shut up and comb your face.'

It had happened after a hard-fought away match, when my stalwart team mates and I had stopped off for a pint or two before splitting up and wending our separate and weary ways home.

It must have been the effect of the full moon because few of my gallant comrades got home that night without incident. In fact few of them got home at all. Those that did wished they hadn't.

Several missed their last trains. Harvey Wallbanger spent the night in a doorway of the YWCA. They wouldn't let him in on account of his not being a member, and wouldn't have passed the medical even if he'd applied. Not with that moustache.

Tactful Tetters was picked up by the Fuzz on being found wandering in charge of a half-empty bottle of Scotch.

'You've been brought here for drinking,' they said at the cop-shop.

'Good,' said Tetters. 'When do we start?'

Young Brookman walked nine miles home, arrived at three in the morning, came in for some lengthy verbal abuse from his Ever Loving after getting into bed with his wellies on, and was sentenced to sleep in the shed.

Scouse Ian, after wandering a few exhausting miles, spied a builder's skip, climbed into it and went to sleep. He was discovered by the vigilant constabulary and escorted to the local nick.

'What's the charge?' he asked.

'Drunk in charge of a skip,' said the desk sergeant.

Ian came off very well. Got a nice warm cell and breakfast in the morning. Pleaded guilty and was fined a fiver.

'I mean to say,' he said afterwards, 'where else could you get bed and breakfast for a fiver at that time of night?'

Poor old Mitch suffered grievous bodily harm.

Missis Mitch, worried by his non-appearance, drove down to the local station to see if he'd made it on the last train.

He had. There he was, lying on a low wall outside the station. Unconscious and with an egg-sized lump on his head, the result of some small miscalculation on de-training. Festooned with tackle and surrounded by a crowd of curious but unsympathetic citizens.

'I was so *ashamed*,' said Missis Mitch next morning.

'Ooh, me head,' said Mitch. 'Could you put some rubber heels on that cat?'

Christopher Robin came the nearest to being sent down for a long stretch. He arrived home to find the house locked and barred. If he had a key he was in no fit state to find it, being extremely tired and emotional.

'She's locked me out,' he thought. And with no more ado bashed in a pane of glass on the front door, stuck his hand through and opened it.

Leaving his gear outside on the step, he went upstairs, rehearsing a few well-chosen words.

In the marital bedroom he was greeted with a sight calculated to strike shock and horror into the stoutest heart. In the bed were a couple, a bloke and a lady person, blissfully kipping.

Christopher was about to take some stern measures when by the light of the moon, he noticed that the furniture was no familiar. Nor was the wallpaper of any pattern he had seen before.

Tippy-toeing down the stairs at the speed of light, he closed the front door quietly behind him, picked up his gear and sho off down the road, where he eventually found his own little love-nest.

'I had a horrible dream,' he said to his Ever Loving next morning. 'I dreamt you'd locked me out and that I'd broken in and found myself in the wrong house.'

Walking down the road a little later, he observed a police car drawn up. The constable, in company with Christopher's very puzzled neighbour, was examining a smashed window in the front door and writing suspicious conclusions in his note-book. Which caused Christopher suddenly to remember an urgent previous engagement in the opposite direction.

* * *

'. . . So you see,' I said to Dearly Beloved some days later, after hearing of all the dreadful happenings. 'Falling asleep on the train was nothing in comparison to what happened to some of the lads. It *must* have been the full moon.'

'Couldn't have had anything to do with the amount you'd all supped, could it?' said Dearly Beloved. (Ooh. Nasty.) 'You must have won the match by a hell of a margin for you all to get so paralytic.'

'Won the match?' I said. 'Who said anything about *winning*?'

But once a year . . .

Dear Uncle Clifford,

It's not really your fault. You were right about the club's Christmas dinner and social evening being a good time for a once-and-for-all reconciliation between Father and Sidney. In theory, nothing could have been better.

What neither Sidney nor I realised, however, was that both the Sludgethorpe Waltonians and the Slagville Piscatorials were holding their Christmas socials on the same night.

Sidney said that he was going to the Waltonians' do no matter what; his loyalties still lay primarily with them. But I pointed out that if he did not attend the Piscatorials' function, Father would never forgive him, and would almost certainly try to have him expelled from the club for disloyalty.

So in the end we compromised: we went to both functions. And, compromises being what they are, ended up by pleasing nobody.

As the Waltonians' meal started earlier than the Piscatorials', we went to that club first. Sidney has lots of friends there, and with them he drank more than he ought before the meal began. During the meal, too, he helped himself lavishly to the wine, reckoning that if he had to face the Piscatorials he needed something to kill the pain.

At the end of the meal the Waltonians' chairman stood up to make a speech, and was not too pleased to see Sidney and myself sneaking out. Took it very personally, he did, and made some very cutting remarks as we left the hall.

We had a hair-raising dash by mini-cab to get to the Piscatorials, where the meal was already underway. My father asked Sidney what he thought he was playing at, getting there when everybody was well into their sautée potatoes and brussels sprouts. Sidney replied to the effect that my father was an interfering old bum and why didn't he belt up?

Father was about to remonstrate when Mother prodded him under the table with her fork. I don't know where she prodded him, but it certainly made his eyes water.

Sidney just toyed with his food, saying that if he had to force any of this Piscatorials' muck down him he'd throw up, but he seemed to enjoy the Piscatorials' wine very much indeed.

By the time the meal ended, Sidney was obviously not himself. When the Piscatorials' chairman rose to make his speech, Sidney demanded that he sit down, shut up, and let everybody get on with some serious supping.

'Why don't you stand over by the wall?' said the chairman. 'That's plastered, too.' I thought that was a bit uncalled for, even though it was not bad for an instant riposte, and it caused Sidney to stand up and shout, 'Sludgethorpe! Sludgethorpe! Rah, rah, rah!'

Father, unmindful of further stabs from Mother's fork, threw himself upon Sidney and they rolled under the table, kicking and gouging. He was joined by several of the more intoxicated Piscatorials, and they gave Sidney a severe thrashing, as well as upsetting the drinks.

Other Piscatorials, who had become friendly with my beloved during his time at the club, and seeing him getting the worst of it, dived to his aid. By now the tables were overturned and all the lady guests had fled the room.

All except Mother, that is. She strode into the struggling mass, stabbing left and right with her fork, pulled Father and several other people off Sidney, and dragged the poor lamb to the door. Here she handed him over to me, with instructions to get him home in a taxi, and barred the way, fork in hand, to would-be pursuers.

. . . My poor Sidney is now in a very bad way, covered in sticking plaster and bandages, and with his ribs strapped up. He has been expelled from the Piscatorials, presented with a huge bill for damage to the hall, and threatened with legal action by several of the members, including Father.

There is an enquiry pending at the Waltonians, too, about

his allegedly discourteous conduct in leaving before the speeches, and bringing the club into disrepute by his conduct at the Piscatorials' function.

Uncle Clifford, I couldn't face another year like this last one. Please tell me that things will improve.

Worried Blue Eyes

Dear Worried Blue Eyes,

Courage, my dear. Take heart. You've had an incident-packed year, that's all, and such incidents are far from rare in a close relationship with an angler.

Remember that next month sees another year. A fresh start. A whole new dawn.

Not that things will improve; in angling family circles they seldom do. But at least you'll be more used to them the second time round.

And dare I suggest that you try to look at things in a less self-centred way? If relationships between anglers and their nearest and dearest ever ran smoothly, there would be no call for advice, no demand for the wisdom and hard-won experience of agony uncles such as myself.

Try thinking of me for a change. God knows, I need the money.

Get up them stairs

I don't seem to be having the luck lately. Since finishing up in the railway siding I had another occasion to arrive home a bit late, owing to some in-depth discussion with Mad Mac and Big McGinty on the day's fishing.

Tired and emotional I may have been, but in full possession of my faculties. I went in by the back door, dumped tackle and clobber in the kitchen, and crept quietly upstairs. Dearly Beloved was deep in slumber, so no probs about interrogation.

On with Superman pyjamas, turn back duvet, slide gently into marital couch. Easy-peasy.

Then the bed collapsed.

Over what followed, I shall draw a veil. Except to say that Dearly Beloved, from her prone position among the wreckage, let fly with some very cutting and personal remarks which included aspersions on my skill as a handyman (me having fixed the wonky bed-leg some months before, and having assured her that all was now well).

However, let the incident be a timely and awful warning to you lads involved in club Yuletide socials and other festive activities. It may not be timely enough: some of you may already have been confined to the doghouse. But for those of you who haven't, here is Uncle Clifford's advice to the Tired and Emotional.

Try to get home under your own steam, i.e. don't trust your mates. Statistics show that nine out of ten mates – especially if Mad Mac and Big McGinty are two of the nine – will do no more than prop you up against the front door, ring the bell and run away. Leaving you to fall in a crumpled heap, possibly with a heaped crump, into the hallway as soon as the door is opened.

That's bad enough, but occasionally the Loved One will throw open the door and flounce straight back upstairs. Leaving you lying there, exposed to the elements and mayhap comatose, with your gear scattered halfway up the street.

Make for the back door. That way you can divest yourself of tackle and gear in the kitchen. On no account try to get upstairs in full clobber. Not only does it make a lot of noise going up, it makes a hell of a lot more coming down when you trip over your waders.

Do not switch on any lights other than those essential to navigation. Which means taking more care than usual to avoid the family pet. You can easily calm down a slobbering dog, and dispose of the cat by a quick heave into the Great Outdoors. But you can't if you've already stepped on them and they're running about yelping or caterwauling.

The budgie, when stepped on, seldom makes a lot of noise on account of being dead. But serves it right: it shouldn't have been out of the cage anyway.

Go upstairs slowly, stepping on the outside of the treads: they squeak less than the middle bits. Make sure you've climbed every last one of the stairs before attempting to step into the bedroom. And if you've got guests, make sure it's the right bedroom.

Mad Mac got home late one Christmas, slipped silently into bed, then realised that the bulk beside him was several times larger than Missis Mac. He switched on the light and – Shock! Horror! Eek! – found himself face to face with his mother-in-law. He'd forgotten that Missis Mac had altered the sleeping arrangements for her dear mama's visit.

Inside the bedroom pay special attention to your orientation, i.e. be sure you're heading in the right direction. Last Christmas a certain person, who shall be nameless, turned right instead of left and walked straight into the wall. It didn't half hurt.

Direction applies to the bed as well. I was perhaps disorientated by walking into the wall, but was very puzzled to find that my head was trapped in what appeared to be folds of material, while my feet were feeling ice cold.

Dearly Beloved, who had been awakened by the struggles, said she didn't wish to pry or anything, and she was sure I had my reasons, but why had I got into bed upside down?

Be sure that you are properly dressed for slumber, i.e. have taken off all your clothes, certainly your wellies, and put on pyjamas. Don't take the easy way out and leave your anorak or shirt on. The pockets could well contain a forgotten spinner, some hook maggots put in there for warmth, or even a half-used bottle of pilchard oil with a loose stopper. Wives on the whole are not keen on sharing the bed with spinners, maggots or pilchard oil.

Neither are they keen on sharing the bed with a turkey, even though it *is* dead. I mention this because Mad Mac once won a turkey in the club Christmas raffle. It was dead, but otherwise intact, feathers and all. All the way home he'd been re-membering not to let go of it, but he should have released it before climbing into bed. The morning spectacle of an un-conscious Mac clutching a 20lb turkey to his bosom did not give Missis Mac the best of starts to the day.

Have the forethought to get a peace offering for your Loved One. But leave the presentation until next day. Wives do not go into ecstasies over being woken at two in the morning to be given a bag of Malteser mis-shapes. Nor do they relish being handed a bunch of flowers still heavy with ice-cold dew from the cemetery. And the list of acceptable presents does *not* in-clude dead pike. I know they're cheaper, but for once hang the expense.

Finally, keep your hands to yourself. And your feet, for that matter. Remember that you will be deep-frozen from the day's exposure to the elements and the journey home. All your good work will be undone if your Ever Loving leaps screaming from the bed at the touch of a corpse-like mitt.

It's no good saying, 'Cold hands, warm heart.' You'll still finish up kipping with the cat on the sofa, wondering what's got into the wife *this* time.

Do it your way

Laydeez an' gennelmen! A little song entitled . . . A little song entitled *The Angler's Farewell to His Conger*. Or *It's a Fine Time to Leave Me, Loose Eel* . . .

That has little or nothing to do with what follows, but I've been trying to get rid of it for weeks. Ta.

Another thing I'm trying to get rid of, to get out of my system altogether, is that song *My Way*. I rate it the yuckiest song since *Deck of Cards* ('I *was* that soldier . . .') but it keeps coming back.

You can't walk into a pub – especially around Christmas, for some reason – without hearing it from the juke box. Or worse, from some euphoric citizen who has a personal message for the world. (The message seems to be that if you do it his way you finish up off key, falling about and spilling beer all over the piano.)

I've been trying to lay the ghost by writing an angler's version of the song. If any of you *must* sing *My Way* at your club's Christmas social, at least you can now express sentiments which bear some relation to the Noble Art. You can make up your own words as well: you're bound to do better than me because I always have trouble making verses scan. As witness:

> *What is an angler?*
> *What has he got?*
> *Apart from pneumonia, rheumatism, arthritis, piles,*
> *   alcoholism and athlete's foot,*
> *Then not a lot . . .*

You can get a few digs in the club officials while you're at it. They always go down well. Except with the club officials. Try:

> *What is a treasurer?*
> *What has he got?*
> *The social funds*

144

Are not a lot.
But if by fits
And then by starts,
He taps the Christmas
Club and Darts,
He'll shout, 'Olé!
'Where's St Tropez?'
And do it his way . . .

Much of the emotion, most of the hassle, almost all the rivalries, jealousies and personal feuds in an angling club, arise from the match activities. For example:

Ah yes, I've fished.
At least I've tried.
And I have had
My share of losin'.
The gallant captain,
Of my team
Has put it down
To late-night boozin' . . .

'I just couldn't understand your performance in the match this morning,' he said. 'I can only think it's the drink.'
'All right,' I said. 'I'll come back when you're sober.'

During the match
He gave a scream:
'You struck too late
'And lost that bream!'
I took the blows
Right od by doze
Ad did id by way . . .

Match fishing is a prime cause of domestic friction, too. At times the Lights of Our Lives have been known to take drastic action to ensure the performance of some household or social task, such as retiling the mother-in-law or being introduced to the kids. ('The little one at the end is Wayne. You've not actually met him yet. Mind you, he *is* only five.')

> *What is a matchman?*
> *What has he got?*
> *If he's chained down,*
> *Then not a lot.*
> *If the wife says, 'Frank,*
> *Stay off that bank,'*
> *He does it no way . . .*

I play it crafty, though, and build up a stock of credits beforehand by helping around the house and being generally creepy. Not that it works every time:

> *Yes, I washed the pots,*
> *Shampooed the cat,*
> *Did all the shopping*
> *And stuff like that.*
> *But if you ask*
> *'Did it work out?'*
> *I'd say I got*
> *Precisely nowt.*
> *She hid the gin*
> *And locked me in*
> *And did it her way . . .*

*   *   *

I feel better for that.

Get on yer bike!

Goods On Board

The hilarious new novel by
SIMON MAYLE

Dear Reader,

I promise you that this book is so witty you'll be reading it
aloud to the nearest traffic warden. You'll need three boxes of
extra-strong hankies for the sad bits. You'll find brilliant new
insights into modern romance.

Besides all this, there's a load of great stuff about motor-
cycling, Life, and what it's like to wear leather.

Basically, reading this is nearly as good as doing a ton down
the South Circular, or a wheelie along the Mall. Go for it!

James

0 7221 5750 9   GENERAL FICTION   £2.50

**The hilarious, heartwarming tales
of a GP in his West Country practice**

SURELY NOT, DOCTOR!

Dr Robert Clifford

Doctor Bob's country practice is in Tadchester on the
Somerset coast, but no one can accuse the town of being
a sleepy little backwater. All human life is there with
its quirks, colour, comedy and richness . . .

There's the absent-minded, incontinent vicar of St
Peter's; the well-known London publisher whose dog
has more taste than most . . . the lady magistrate who
travels for miles for a doctor with warm hands and
the packet of suppositories which prompts a bomb scare!

It all goes to show that truth can be so much stranger
than fiction . . .

BIOGRAPHY/HUMOUR   0 7221 2386 8   £1.95

Don't miss Dr Robert Clifford's

**JUST HERE, DOCTOR!
NOT THERE, DOCTOR!
WHAT NEXT, DOCTOR?
OH DEAR, DOCTOR!
LOOK OUT, DOCTOR!**

Also available in Sphere Books

The Freakiest, Funniest Book About Animals – *Ever!*

ODDBODS!

Bill Garnett

FIRST THERE WAS *THE NAKED APE*. THEN CAME *THE NAKED NUN*... NOW – AT LAST – THE NAKED TRUTH!

There are creatures that walk this planet which:

* *Bathe in acid*
* *Baffle Radar*
* *Turn into plants*
* *Do business – and have sex – without their heads*

You'll find them – and many others even stranger – in *ODDBODS!*

IT'S EVERYTHING YOU NEVER WANTED TO KNOW ABOUT ANIMALS – BUT WILL BE STAGGERED TO HEAR!

HUMOUR/NON-FICTION   0 7221 3809 1   £1.75

A THOROUGHLY LEWD COLLECTION OF EXCEEDINGLY RUDE RHYMES!!

Ribald, ingenious, hilariously blue – this side-splitting selection of bawdy limericks will have you reeling with riotous laughter and mirth-filled merriment. There's Adam complacently stroking his madam . . . Irene who made an offering quite obscene . . . Hyde who fell down a privy and died . . . the young fellow of Kent who had a peculiar bent . . . the brainy professor named Zed who dreamed of a buxom co-ed . . . and many, many more!

0 7221 1297 1   HUMOUR £1.95

A selection of bestsellers from Sphere

FICTION

WANDERLUST	Danielle Steel	£3.50 ☐
LADY OF HAY	Barbara Erskine	£3.95 ☐
BIRTHRIGHT	Joseph Amiel	£3.50 ☐
THE SECRETS OF HARRY BRIGHT	Joseph Wambaugh	£2.95 ☐
CYCLOPS	Clive Cussler	£3.50 ☐

FILM AND TV TIE-IN

INTIMATE CONTACT	Jacqueline Osborne	£2.50 ☐
BEST OF BRITISH	Maurice Sellar	£8.95 ☐
SEX WITH PAULA YATES	Paula Yates	£2.95 ☐
RAW DEAL	Walter Wager	£2.50 ☐

NON-FICTION

AS TIME GOES BY: THE LIFE OF INGRID BERGMAN	Laurence Leamer	£3.95 ☐
BOTHAM	Don Mosey	£3.50 ☐
SOLDIERS	John Keegan & Richard Holmes	£5.95 ☐
URI GELLER'S FORTUNE SECRETS	Uri Geller	£2.50 ☐
A TASTE OF LIFE	Julie Stafford	£3.50 ☐

All Sphere books are available at your local bookshop or newsagent, or can be ordered direct from the publisher. Just tick the titles you want and fill in the form below.

Name_____

Address_____

_____

Write to Sphere Books, Cash Sales Department, P.O. Box 11, Falmouth, Cornwall TR10 9EN

Please enclose a cheque or postal order to the value of the cover price plus:

UK: 60p for the first book, 25p for the second book and 15p for each additional book ordered to a maximum charge of £1.90.

OVERSEAS & EIRE: £1.25 for the first book, 75p for the second book and 28p for each subsequent title ordered.

BFPO: 60p for the first book, 25p for the second book plus 15p per copy for the next 7 books, thereafter 9p per book.

Sphere Books reserve the right to show new retail prices on covers which may differ from those previously advertised in the text elsewhere, and to increase postal rates in accordance with the P.O.